The South Pennine Ring
A Seventy-Mile Circuit of Canals

including
- The Rochdale Canal
- The Huddersfield Narrow Canal
- The Huddersfield Broad Canal

and connecting parts of
- The Ashton Canal
- The Calder & Hebble Navigation

John Lower

The Hallamshire Press
A Richlow Guide

Text © 1998 Interleaf Productions Limited
Photographs and Maps © 1998 John Lower

Published by The Hallamshire press
The Hallamshire Press is an imprint of
Interleaf Productions Limited
Broom Hall
Sheffield S10 2DR
England

Typeset by Interleaf Productions Limited
Printed in Singapore

British Library Cataloguing in Publication Data

Lower, John
    The south Pennine ring: a seventy-mile circuit of canals.
    - (Richlow guides)
    1. Canals - England - Pennine Chain - Guidebooks 2. Walking -
    England - Pennine Chain - Guidebooks 3. Pennine Chain
    (England) - Guidebooks
    I. Title
    914.2'8'04859

ISBN 1-874718-37-7

Contents

Acknowledgements

I wish to thank the many people who have helped with the information in this guide, especially:
- Barbara, Richard and Andrew Lower for boating and walking with me;
- Dick Booth for always being about the Rochdale Canal, even on his days off;
- Tony Balfour (*The Cheshire Junk*) who, when boating single-handed down the Ashton Locks, let me play with his lock-handle;
- Christopher and Judy, Paul and Sarah Clegg (*Balador*) for being good company on the Rochdale;
- Mike Catchpole, Paul Freemont, Howard Mann;
- Nigel and Sue Stevens of Shire Cruisers
    and
- Christine Richardson for trusting me with the Richlow title.
Thanks also to the canal restorers for their foresight, dedication and hard graft.

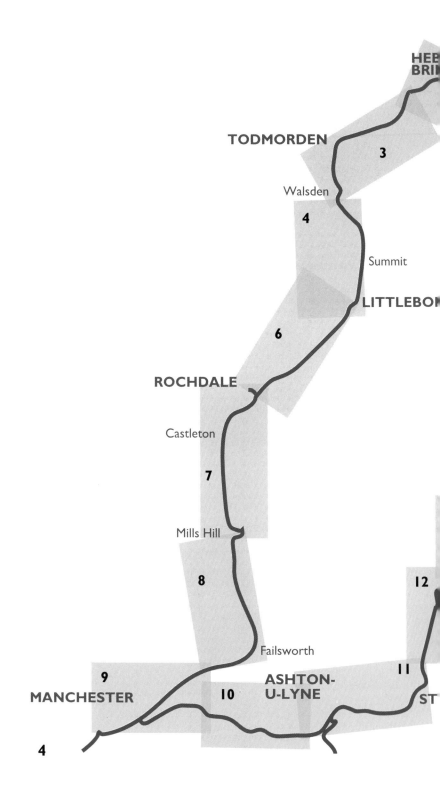

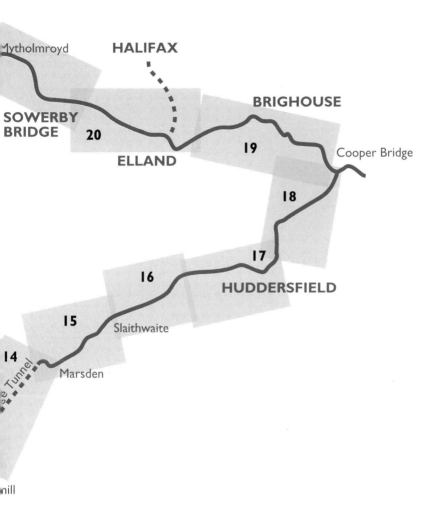

Mytholmroyd

HALIFAX

SOWERBY BRIDGE

BRIGHOUSE

20

ELLAND

19

Cooper Bridge

18

17

16

HUDDERSFIELD

15

Slaithwaite

14

Marsden

e Tunnel

nill

Distances (in miles)

Rochdale Canal

Sowerby Bridge																		
5½	Hebden Bridge																	
10	4½	Todmorden																
15½	10	5½	Littleborough															
20	14½	10	4½	Rochdale														
24	18½	14	8½	4	Mills Hill													
27	21½	17	11½	7	3	Failsworth												
31	25½	21	15½	11	7	4	Dale Street, Manchester											
37		*Ashton Canal*					6	Portland Basin, Ashton-under-Lyne										
38½							1½	Stalybridge										
42		*Huddersfield Narrow Canal*					5	3½	Greenfield									
45½							8½	7	3½	Diggle								
49							12	10½	7	3½	Marsden							
52							15	13½	10	6½	3	Slaithwaite						
57							20	18½	15	11½	8	5	Aspley Basin, Huddersfield					
60						*Huddersfield Broad*							3	Cooper Bridge				
62						*Calder & Hebble*								2	Brighouse			
64½														4½	2½	Elland		
68½	63	58½	53	48½	44½	41½	37½	31½	30	26½	23	19½	16½	11½	8½	6½	4	Sowerby Bridge

Key to Maps

fb	= footbridge		**PH**	= public house
pb	= pipe bridge		**T**	= telephone
MS10	= milestone (10 miles)		**LB**	= letter box
VM	= visitor mooring		**L**	= launderette
↰**60**	= turning point for 60 ft boat		**FC**	= fish & chip shop or takeaway
W	= water point		**GS**	= general stores
WC	= boaters' toilet		**GP**	= garage petrol
ED	= Elsan disposal		**WC**	= public toilet
RD	= rubbish disposal		**CP**	= public car park
			PO	= post office
bridge name ✕ — no access at bridge			**MUS**	= museum
			⇌	= railway station
			news	= newsagent
			ℹ	= tourist information

Introduction

This book contains all you need to know to explore the canals of the South Pennines, whether by boat or on foot. A watery 'Ring of Roses' includes the Rochdale Canal and the Huddersfield Narrow and Broad Canals. The Ashton Canal and part of the Calder & Hebble Navigation are included to make up a circuit of almost seventy miles, and there is a section on the long-derelict Halifax Canal.

The journey is one of extreme contrasts: high moors of the Pennines; picturesque tourist centres such as Hebden Bridge and Uppermill; fascinating woollen town heritage of Huddersfield and Halifax; the urban excitement that is central Manchester. Along the route is Britain's longest canal tunnel at Standedge, and there are many fascinating examples of industrial archaeology and locks, more than 200 of them! **The Huddersfield Narrow and Rochdale Canals are the subject of major restoration schemes which, when completed, will make Britain's premier canal ring.**

This comprehensive guide includes easy-to-follow maps, logical ordering of information, details of the history of each navigation and is well illustrated by full colour photography. *The South Pennine Ring* is the fourth book in the 'Richlow' series and has been thoroughly researched on foot and by boat.

The author is a local canal society member, enthusiast and boat owner who regularly writes for the waterway magazines and gives illustrated talks throughout the area. He has also been extensively involved in canal restoration.

Please note: Restoration work is in progress on the Rochdale and Huddersfield Narrow Canals with a view to completion by 2001. In the meantime, construction work may close sections of the towpath or limit public access. Respect these closures — they are for your own safety.

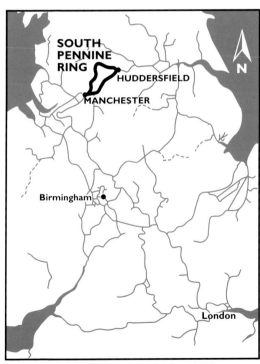

The Connected Waterways of England and Wales

Interesting Things to Look Out for along the Waterways

½-mile post and 100-yard marker (see page 108) at Kirklees Locks

Milestone, Huddersfield Narrow Canal

Milestone, Rochdale Canal. Mileposts were an important feature of canals: they were used to calculate the tolls due from the movement of goods.

Remains of towrope roller, Elland

Grooves in the stone caused by the towrope and metal protecting strip to the bridge parapet: Huddersfield Broad Canal

Swing bridge base, Mossley (see page 78)

Remains of crane, Stalybridge

Milepost, Rochdale Canal

Below: A loop in the end of the towrope was dropped over this 'horn' and the rope passed round a pulley on the mast. This gave the horse two-to-one advantage to start the boat. As the boat left the lock, the loop fell off and a peg in the rope held in the pulley (Rochdale Canal Locks)

Ground paddle vent, Huddersfield Narrow Canal

A capstan roller, round which a chain passed: connected to a plug in the canal bed to let out the water (Huddersfield Canals)

9

1. Lapwing; 2. Goldfinch; 3. Kingfisher; 4. Heron (pictures not to scale)

Wildlife

Crossing high through the Pennine hills, the Huddersfield Narrow Canal and the Rochdale Canal form important watery wildlife corridors. They stretch from the pure upland moors, running through deep wooded valleys and penetrate the major conurbations on either side. They bring clean water down into the valleys and allow birds, animals, fish and plants to migrate.

Passing through such diverse landscapes, the boater and walker can expect to see a full range of flora and fauna, often at close quarters. Obvious are the swans, mallard ducks and Canada geese — in summer swallows skim over the water morning and evening — but now look more closely. When moored in Sowerby Bridge Basin, I watched a brilliant blue kingfisher fishing from my bow rope. Moorhens with their red beak paddled across as we headed up the Rochdale Canal. Tall, long-legged herons stood patiently in the water margin waiting to spear a fish or a frog, and sailed majestically into the air on the approach of the boat, usually to execute a wide circle and return when the boat had passed.

Moored in the deep wooded valley above Hebden Bridge, it was possible to hear rather than see the variety of birdlife. I went to sleep to the sound of owls and awoke early to the drumming of woodpeckers and the harsh cry of a jay. Spotted flycatchers, various warblers, chaffinches, bullfinches and goldfinches can be seen together with the usual garden robins, thrushes and blackbirds. On the tree trunks are wrens, tits and tree creepers. The sound of the cuckoo booms across the valley. Hidden here are foxes, hedgehogs and badgers. Bats can be seen flitting among the trees and low over the water at twilight, in search of insects. Grey squirrels thrive and will occasionally be seen swimming across the canal.

The stony banks of the canal are busy with bobbing wagtails and dippers, and water voles swim busily across or dive with a loud 'plop' if disturbed. These charming little creatures were once very common, but now are becoming endangered.

Higher up the valley, the landscape changes to open fields and wild moorland. Flocks of rooks and starlings are seen, while there are rabbits in abundance. A mad March hare is an impressive sight. In summer the valley echoes with the plaintive voices of the lapwing (peewit), curlew and snipe. Up on the rocky crags, merlin, kestrel and kite are king. The reservoirs provide a resting place for migrant birds: geese, waders and even divers. Walking round the reservoir often disturbs grouse, which whizz into the air shrieking their noisy 'go back' cry. In summer, the sky is busy high overhead with the erratic flight and pretty singing of the skylark.

Many other creatures can be seen along the wildlife corridor. After years of gross pollution in the lower reaches, water quality continues annually to improve. I was lucky to see an otter swimming in the river at the rear of British Car Auctions below Brighouse. Mink are also beginning to populate the area.

Improvement in quality of the lower rivers has also resulted in the growth of coarse fishing for perch, roach, tench, bream and pike. In the upland canal lengths, grayling and brown and rainbow trout thrive in the pure water.

Rollers across the river at Anchor Pit Flood Lock prevents boats from being swept over the weir, but do not trap flood debris.

Unique Calder & Hebble handspike in operation, seen here at Elland Lock

Navigational Information

All the waterways included in this book were built at different times by different companies, giving each a distinctive style and flavour, a delight for the canal enthusiast. The boater must be aware that the canals were built to three different gauges, and that a range of navigational equipment is required to work the locks, etc. Different licences are also required for the Rochdale Canal.

At the time of writing, the Ashton Canal, the Huddersfield Broad Canal and the Calder & Hebble Navigation are all fully navigable. The Rochdale Canal is navigable through the nine locks at Manchester and from Sowerby Bridge to Littleborough and the Huddersfield Narrow Canal from Ashton-under-Lyne to Stalybridge. Short stretches of the Huddersfield Narrow Canal are available to trailboaters and further stretches of both this and the Rochdale Canal will become available as restoration proceeds.

Hopefully, the entire ring will be fully navigable in 2001.

Navigation Authorities

A licence is required to navigate the waterways as follows:

Rochdale Canal, Sowerby Bridge to Littleborough and beyond as restoration proceeds: Rochdale Canal Trust 01422 844990. Short-term licences can be purchased on the day at Tuel Lane Lock.

Rochdale Canal, Manchester Nine Locks: Rochdale Canal Company 0161 236 2456 (at the time of writing, but this may change to Rochdale Canal Trust as the restoration scheme succeeds). Permit for single passage can be purchased on the day but cheaper if booked in advance.

A British Waterways Canals Cruising Licence is required for the *Ashton Canal, Huddersfield Narrow Canal, Huddersfield Broad Canal and the Calder & Hebble Navigation*. (Bridgewater Canal Licence holders can obtain this at reduced cost from The Manchester Ship Canal Company; see page 126).

Bridgewater Canal: British Waterways licence holders can transit the Bridgewater Canal for seven days at no cost under a reciprocal arrangement. Non BW licence holders will need to apply to the Manchester Ship Canal Company; see page 126.

Recommended Maximum Craft Dimensions

Rochdale Canal, Sowerby Bridge to Littleborough: 72 ft length × 14 ft 2 in beam × 7 ft 9 in headroom. (*Note:* Copperas Bridge at Walsden is considerably lower than all others on the navigation and the headroom can vary considerably with the water level on the short pound.)

Rochdale Canal Manchester Nine Locks: 72 ft length × 14 ft 2 in beam × 9 ft headroom.

Ashton Canal and Huddersfield Narrow Canal: 70 ft length × 7 ft beam × 6 ft headroom.

Huddersfield Broad Canal and Calder & Hebble Navigation: 57 ft 5 in length × 14 ft 2 in beam × 9 ft 4 in headroom. (*Note:* with care, narrow boats up to 60 ft can navigate these waterways.)

On completion of restoration, a narrow boat or cruiser not exceeding 60 ft length × 7 ft beam × 6 ft headroom will be able to circumnavigate the South Pennine Ring.

Navigation Equipment

Lock-key, (lock handle or windlass). A standard short-throw lock-key will operate the narrow locks. A longer throw-key is advisable to operate the heavier paddles of the broad locks.

Handspike. A wooden handle like a capstan-bar used to operate some paddles on the Calder & Hebble Navigation. Purpose-made handspikes can be purchased from chandleries or the British Waterways offices at Castleford. I purchased a 1.2 metre length of 75 mm × 50 mm timber from a timber yard which is a cheaper and more readily available alternative. (Don't believe the boater who tells you can manage without a handspike!)

Handcuff key: a small 'T'-shaped key used to unlock the anti-vandal locks on the Rochdale, Aston and Huddersfield Narrow Canals.

'Watermate' or BW sanitary station key: used not only to gain access to sanitary stations but

Cycle lock-ups are provided at most stations in the West Yorkshire area.

Walking at Diggle

Fishing: Elland Basin

also to operate movable bridges such as the Locomotive Bridge at Huddersfield or Guillotine lockgates such as at Salterhebble and Todmorden. Also opens some car park barriers. Available from BW or boatyards.

Anchor: should be carried for the river sections of the Calder & Hebble Navigation.

Speed Limit

Speed limit: 4 mph. However, boaters should not navigate at speeds that cause excessive wash and should never cause a breaking wash. Slow down when passing moored craft.

Slipways

There are a number of slipways around the ring that remain locked, private or unusable, or the owners just can't be bothered with visitors. Surprisingly, I could not locate one on the Greater Manchester side. Here are the ones that I have found readily available:

> *Sowerby Bridge (Shire Cruisers) 01422 832712*
>
> *Hebden Bridge Marina (Rochdale Canal Trust) 01422 844990*
>
> *Uppermill (Brownhill Visitor Centre) 01457 872598*
>
> *Slaithwaite (Huddersfield Canal Society) 0161 339 1332*

Other Users

Walking

Towpaths are shown on the maps and are generally in good condition. However, diversions are presently required on sections of infilled canal at Manchester, Rochdale Queensway, Failsworth, Stalybridge and Huddersfield until restoration is completed. In addition, a diversion is required for the river section of the Calder & Hebble below Brighouse where the towpath is not a public right of way and is badly overgrown.

Boat Lane over Standedge Tunnel and the Rochdale Canal Reservoirs Walk are exposed high-level walks over remote moorland and the walker's attention is drawn to the need for stout footwear, weatherproof clothing and the safety warnings included on the appropriate pages.

Certain urban areas, especially in Central Manchester, may be threatening to the timid lone walker (though your intrepid researcher did it alone). Make your walking here more social and take a friend.

Railways follow most of the route and frequent stations make the planning of one-way walks a simple matter. There are also good bus services, especially in the Calder and Colne Valleys. See public transport, page 122.

Cycling

Permits are required to cycle on the canal towpaths as follows:

Rochdale Canal, Sowerby Bridge to Manchester. A permit is currently available from the Rochdale Canal Company, 75 Dale Street, Manchester M1 2HG, 0161 236 2456, at a cost of £5 per annum. (This may change with the take-over of the canal by the Rochdale Canal Trust.)

British Waterways Canals. A free national permit is currently issued by any of the Waterways Managers' Offices. Cycling is presently permitted on the Ashton Canal (0161 427 1079) and the Huddersfield Broad Canal (01977 554351). Cycling is permitted on certain lengths of the Huddersfield Narrow Canal (01484 844298). Cycling is not permitted along the Calder & Hebble Navigation.

Cyclists should treat towpaths with respect and be prepared to give way to other users. Look out for pedestrians and anglers and their tackle.

Lock No. 1, Sowerby Bridge

Rochdale Canal

Edward Kilner Lock, Brearley

History of the Rochdale Canal

Three Famous Engineers

At the same time as proposals were being made for the Leeds & Liverpool Canal, residents of Halifax, Hebden Bridge, Todmorden and Rochdale suggested a shorter route across the Pennines, connecting Manchester on the Bridgewater Canal with the Calder & Hebble Navigation at Sowerby Bridge. James Brindley was called to advise and carried out a survey for a narrow canal in 1766. No further action seems to have been taken.

In 1791, canal mania was sweeping the country and another survey was authorised, this time by John Rennie. Acts of Parliament were applied for in 1792 and 1793 but failed due to opposition from mill owners, especially in the Calder Valley, who feared for their water supply and also from the Manchester, Bolton & Bury Canal who proposed an alternative route linking to their canal at Bury. An Act was finally obtained in 1794 with the assistance of William Jessop, but Parliament insisted on a broad waterway.

The First Trans-Pennine Route

The Rochdale Canal was opened throughout in 1804, seven years ahead of the Huddersfield Narrow Canal and twelve in front of the Leeds & Liverpool. It was an immediate success.

Railways

The opening of the Liverpool & Manchester Railway in 1829 initially brought increased trade to the canal, but the opening of the Manchester & Leeds Railway on a parallel route in 1841 was in direct competition. Cutting of toll rates began.

The canal was leased to the railway company from 1855 until 1888, when it was at its busiest. It now returned to the canal company who set up their own carrying fleet. It was not the railways that brought about the demise, but the First World War and the introduction of the motor lorry. The last boat through was in 1937 and the canal was legally abandoned (except the nine locks in Manchester) in 1952.

The Rochdale Nine and the Cheshire Ring

The Rochdale Canal Company was not nationalised in 1948 and remains successful to the present day, some major sources of income being sale of water, car parking and land rental. In 1964, the company could see no future for the remaining navigation beneath Manchester city centre and proposed to close it for redevelopment.

A protest was organised by the Inland Waterways Association whereby a working narrow boat was forced through the nine decrepit locks to carry out a contract at Piccadilly. It took twelve days and involved shifting tons of rubbish and removing scaffolding from beneath Rodwell Tower, then under construction over the canal and Lock 85. As a result, the Canal Company agreed to keep the locks open as long as there remained a legal right of navigation on the connecting Ashton Canal.

The locks became part of the popular Cheshire Ring of cruising waterways with the reopening of the Ashton Canal in 1974. Subsequent improvements have been carried out, many promoted by the now defunct Central Manchester Development Corporation.

Restoration

Rochdale Canal Society was formed in 1974 and campaigned for navigation over the Pennines once more. Volunteers held work parties and restored Longlees Lock during the 1970s. The local authorities joined the campaign with work commencing on the Todmorden–Hebden Bridge section and also at Littleborough in 1982, using job creation schemes.

Perhaps the biggest challenge to the society was the proposed M66 Manchester Outer Ring Road which would have irreversibly obliterated a section at Chadderton. A 'Big-Dig' was held, also a boat rally and a spirited campaign at the public inquiry, resulting in the motorway plans being altered to include through navigation.

Restoration has continued through the Rochdale Canal Trust, a partnership of the society and all the riparian local authorities. With the reopening of Tuel Lane Lock in 1996, almost half the canal is once again connected to the national system, with much work carried out on the remainder.

Map 1: *Rochdale Canal*
Sowerby Bridge to Brearley
$3\frac{1}{2}$ miles

The magnificent Calderdale landscape comprises a wide valley bottom, with road, railway, river and canal, while the steep hillsides lined with stone walls and dotted with farmhouses rise up to a top layer of wild moorland.

The junction of the Rochdale Canal with the Calder & Hebble Navigation has been named Kirkham Turn in memory of Ralph Kirkham, a tireless local waterway campaigner, chairman of Calder Navigation Society and founder member of the Rochdale Canal Society.

Formerly, there were four locks on the Rochdale Canal at Sowerby Bridge, but the top two were filled in for a road improvement scheme in the late sixties. Now a new curved tunnel carries the canal beneath the new road alignment. Tuel Lane Lock has a rise of 19'6", the deepest in the country. Because of its thirst for water, two sets of bottom gates have been fitted, the outer ones at the standard Rochdale Canal length, and the inner ones (which are usually used) at the shorter Calder & Hebble length. All the locks on the canal were originally fitted with gate pockets to allow water-saving intermediate gates, and many can still be seen: it is thought that only Lock 1 ever had them fitted.

Tuel Lane Lock was opened on 3 May 1996. Shortage of space means that some of its lock-gates do not have balance beams, but are operated by gearing instead. Above the lock, the moorings are very convenient for shopping.

Leaving Sowerby Bridge, the canal is hemmed in by a cliff on one hand and tall mills on the other. Then suddenly it is on a narrow ledge held up by a massive stone retaining wall, with views up to Sowerby village high on the valley side opposite. Sowerby Long Bridge is really a tunnel through a rocky bluff.

Longbottom Bridge had been infilled as an access to Sagar Richard's mill and has been rebuilt in original style and widened using steel corrugated tubing. Where the channel is narrow near milepost 2, it has been rebuilt from a much narrower channel built to give the factory more land — a similar channel is still extant at Rochdale.

Luddenden Foot is an ideal rest point or overnight mooring, with small shops and three pubs. The multi-storey buildings that back onto the canal look like conventional two-storey buildings from the road, showing the steepness of the hillside and that land is at a premium in the valley.

By Ellen Royd Bridge is a towpath-side spillway, designed to protect the canal from flooding. At $2\frac{1}{2}$ miles, this is a long pound (pound is the distance between locks) by Rochdale Canal standards. Edward Kilner Lock is named after a long-serving solicitor and secretary of the Rochdale Canal Company who lived in nearby Brearley Hall at one time. Brearley is another pleasant stopping place with nearby friendly hostelry and pleasant walks into the woodland above.

At Moderna Bridge, another new steel tube bridge has been built on the site of a swing bridge, to carry traffic to an industrial estate.

Navigation Notes

Tuel Lane Lock
Tuel Lane Lock is operated by a lock-keeper (tel 01422 316678). It is not open every day, so check working hours in advance. Under no circumstances enter the tunnel below the lock without the permission of the lock-keeper: turbulence from lock emptying could cause a serious accident to a boat in the tunnel.

Follow the lock-keeper's instructions. Tuel Lane Lock is fitted with vertical stainless steel bars in the lock walls; mooring ropes should be looped round these and held by a crew member while ascending or descending.

Rochdale Canal Licence
Rochdale Canal licences of different durations are available for a fee from the lock-keeper or in advance from the Rochdale Canal Trust at Callis Mill (see page 126).

Towpath Notes:
Good throughout. There is no towpath through Tuel Lane Tunnel — use the 'pelican-crossing' to cross busy Wharf Street and head round the top side of the Lock Keeper's Tavern.

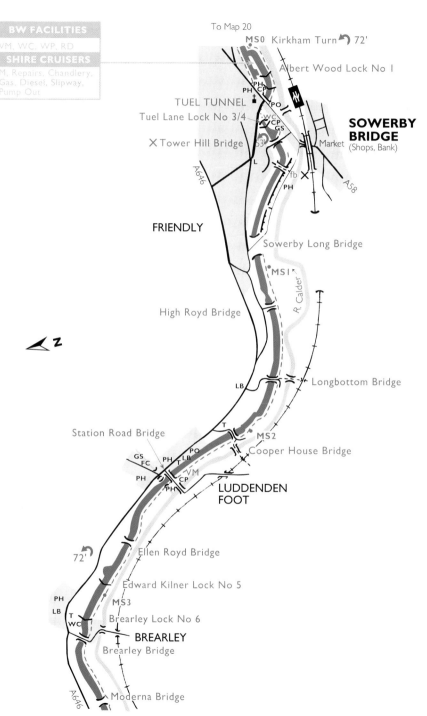

To Map 20

BW FACILITIES
VM, WC, WP, RD

SHIRE CRUISERS
M, Repairs, Chandlery,
Gas, Diesel, Slipway,
Pump Out

MS0 Kirkham Turn ↰ 72'

Albert Wood Lock No 1

PH CP
PO

TUEL TUNNEL
Tuel Lane Lock No 3/4

WC
CP
GS

SOWERBY BRIDGE
(Shops, Bank)

✕ Tower Hill Bridge

Market

53'

L

fb ✕

PH

FRIENDLY

Sowerby Long Bridge

MS1

R. Calder

High Royd Bridge

↖ Z

LB

Longbottom Bridge

T

MS2

Station Road Bridge

GS
FC

PH T

PO
LB

VM

PH

CP

Cooper House Bridge

LUDDENDEN FOOT

72' ↰

Ellen Royd Bridge

Edward Kilner Lock No 5

PH
LB

MS3

T
WC

Brearley Lock No 6

BREARLEY
Brearley Bridge

A646

Moderna Bridge

To Map 2

19

Visitor mooring at Luddenden Foot

A walk through Tuel Tunnel, just before the lock was opened

Tuel Lane Lock

Brearley

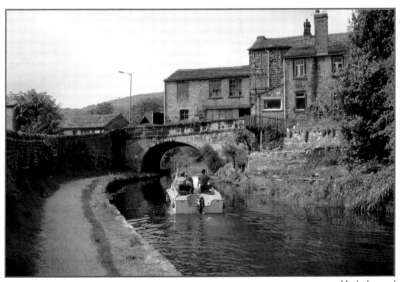

Mytholmroyd

Map 2: *Rochdale Canal*

Mytholmroyd and Hebden Bridge

3½ miles

At Halifax Road Bridge a building spans the canal as part of the bridge structure. There are moorings next to the White Lion for shopping in Mytholmroyd, (pronounced 'My-tham-royd'). Midgley Road Bridge was built in 1986 to replace an embankment. There is an attractive grouping of buildings at Redacre Bridge with the stone-mullioned Redacre House and the canalside Redacre Mill.

Walkley's Clogs is a major tourist destination which has grown up in Britain's only surviving clog mill, just across the road from the canal. Admission is free for shopping, which, besides clogs, includes an all-year Christmas and Easter experience ('The Enchanted Wood'), craft and specialist shops and a cafe. There is a charge for a passport to visit the various exhibitions such as clog manufacture, 'The Land of the Honey Bee' and the 'Cragg Vale Coiners' — the story of local coin counterfeiters.

Fallingroyd Tunnel is the largest of three major blockages in Calderdale that were cleared and reopened on 21 November 1986. It is interesting to watch the horse-drawn trip boat being legged through here. At the clog mill moorings and at several locks, a tethering post has been provided for the boat horse. Beneath Station Road Bridge a roller protects the stonework from the towline.

Unlike all the others along the line, Hebden Bridge Railway Station is a pretty picture. It has been restored to its former glory with all the buildings in use, glass in the canopies, flowers on the platforms and even a buffet in the parcels room.

Hebden Bridge grew up around the river crossing. The stone bridge was built in 1510 replacing an earlier wooden one, while the original town mill is now the Innovation shop. The tourist information centre is an excellent starting point to find out more about the area. With the decline in the traditional industries, the town was falling into decline in the sixties — the resurgence of the town has gone hand in hand with the restoration of the canal, with arts and crafts flourishing in the many small shops.

Hebden Bridge, the self-styled 'Pennine Centre', presents a very attractive face to the canal. The canalside park through was the venue of the Inland Waterways Association's National Trailboat Festival in 1990. The marina has been created on the site of a derelict garage and is a venue for the local tradition of Pace-Egging: on Good Friday, mummers play the story of St George and the Dragon through the town, a moral tale of good triumphing over evil.

Blackpit Lock leads directly into the substantial aqueduct over the River Calder. The canal sneaks out of Hebden Bridge past the Hebble End Craft Centre and through the two Stubbing Locks complete with lock cottage. Beyond Stubbing Wharf with its pub and moorings, the valley becomes much narrower with steep wooded hillsides on either hand. Canal and river are only separated by the towpath.

A waterfall cascades into the large pool below Rawden Mill Lock, a popular mooring for the nearby pub. The factory alongside the lock is Callis Mill, workshops of the Rochdale Canal Trust and lockgates have been made here not just for the Rochdale Canal, but for canals all over the country.

The Pennine Way crosses the canal at Callis Lock; at the end of the day weary hikers can be seen walking the towpath into Hebden Bridge in search of accommodation.

Walking Country

Leaving the canal and ascending the steep valley sides, there are many excellent walks. Before the sixteenth century, most of the population lived high on the valley sides, avoiding the marshy valley bottom. Heptonstall is one such ancient hilltop village and weaving community, little changed. The new church (1854) is a landmark for miles around, but the ruins of the old church dating back to 1260, and which was struck by lightning, still stand alongside. The octagonal Methodist church is thought to be the oldest one still in use. It opened in 1764 and John Wesley preached here on more than one occasion. Descending back to Hebden Bridge, the rows of later, four-decker, back-to-back mill houses are terraced up the hillside.

Hardcastle Crags, a wooded valley owned by the National Trust, is another popular venue for walkers.

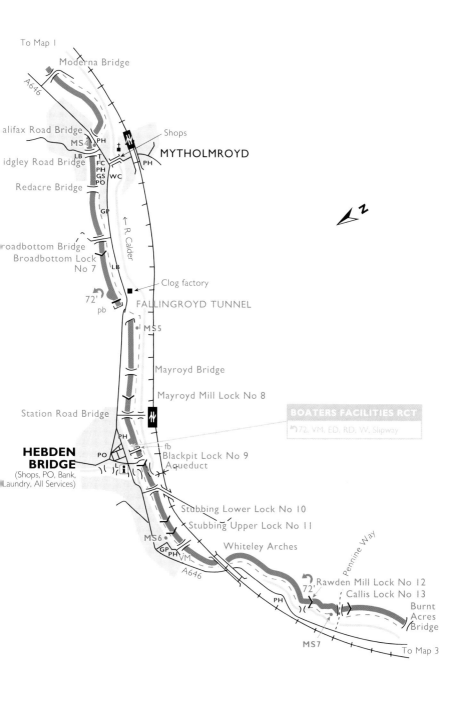

To Map 1
Moderna Bridge
A646
alifax Road Bridge
MS4 PH
idgley Road Bridge
LB T FC PH GS PO
Shops
MYTHOLMROYD
PH
WC
Redacre Bridge
GP
← R. Calder
roadbottom Bridge
Broadbottom Lock No 7
LB
72' pb
Clog factory
FALLINGROYD TUNNEL
MS5
Mayroyd Bridge
Mayroyd Mill Lock No 8

Station Road Bridge
PH
HEBDEN BRIDGE
(Shops, PO, Bank, Laundry, All Services)
PO
fb
Blackpit Lock No 9
Aqueduct

Stubbing Lower Lock No 10
Stubbing Upper Lock No 11
MS6
GP PH VM
A646
Whiteley Arches
Pennine Way
72'
Rawden Mill Lock No 12
Callis Lock No 13
Burnt Acres Bridge
PH
MS7
To Map 3

23

Navigation Notes

Fallingroyd Tunnel

Go slow: Fallingroyd Tunnel is built on a curve so you cannot see craft coming towards you, especially the unpowered trip boat. The curved shape makes it possible to catch the cabin sides on the tunnel roof; keep crew off the gunnels or cabin top. Narrow boats could pass with care in the tunnel, but it is definitely not recommended.

Horse-Drawn Trip Boat

A horse-drawn trip boat operates usually between Walkley's Clogs and Hebden Bridge, but can be encountered at other places. Please take extra care when passing. Pass on the side away from the towpath to avoid fouling the towline. Remember, it has no brakes and cannot stop. It is legged by the crew through Fallingroyd Tunnel. At Hebden Bridge try to moor on the offside visitor moorings.

Stubbing Upper Lock 11 is to be left empty.

Towpath Notes

Good condition throughout. There is no towpath through Fallingroyd Tunnel; please take care when crossing the busy main road.

The towpath changes sides at Blackpit Lock.

Fallingroyd Tunnel

Horse-drawn trip boat at Mayroyd Mill Lock

Redacre House

Mytholmroyd

Moderna Bridge: contrast with the picture on page 66

National Trailboat Festival 1990

Hebden Bridge

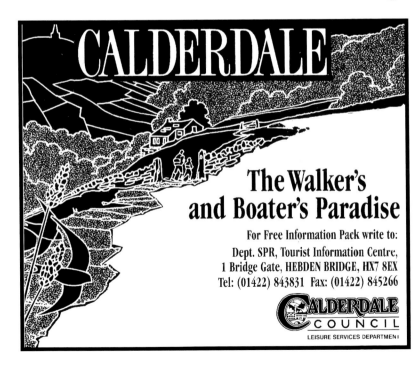

Marina

27

Map 3: *Rochdale Canal*
Callis to Todmorden and Walsden
5 miles

The valley continues narrow and wooded. The locksides are planted with daffodils which provide a brilliant display in spring. Below Shawplains Lock, Pickwell & Arnold have set up their boat-building and boat-hire business in an old mill, specialising in building broad-beam craft. From Shawplains is the shortest walk up to Stoodley Pike (below) and the village of Mankinholes.

At Lob Mill Lock there is a 'pinch-point' in the valley leaving little room for the transport routes to get through. Here there are wild rhododendrons adding their beauty to the landscape.

Modern housing and industry marks the approach to Todmorden. A new marina has been created by Baltimore Boats who operate moorings and hire boats and maintain the sanitary station. Just beyond, there is a gate through the towpath wall giving convenient access to a Cooperative superstore.

Looking forward and back, two significant follies can be seen. In front stands Dobroyd Castle. It was built as a 'job creation scheme' in the 1860s. Behind, prominent on a ridge, stands Stoodley Pike: 120 feet high, it was built in 1814 to commemorate the surrender of Paris to the allies after the Napoleonic Wars. It fell down in 1854 and had to be rebuilt. Climb up there — there is an excellent view from the balcony.

For centuries, the border between Yorkshire and Lancashire ran through Todmorden; indeed the impressive Town Hall originally stood in both counties. Originally this was a woollen town, but with the arrival of the Rochdale Canal and the new-fangled machinery, it quickly changed over to cotton. There is a huge variety of styles of architecture to be seen, all built in local stone.

Today Todmorden is a convenient place for shopping and there are markets every day from Wednesday to Sunday.

At Todmorden Lock a guillotine gate has replaced the bottom lockgates as, following road-widening, there was insufficient room for mitred gates. On the lockside, an old stone milepost has been incorporated into the flower beds. Beyond is the Great Wall of Todmorden, a massive, plain unbuttressed structure rising directly out of the canal, built to support the railway goods yard above.

Beyond Todmorden the locks come thick and fast in a determined effort to reach Summit. The landscape is more wild, with heather and gorse reaching down to the canal bank. At Gauxholme the railway crosses and re-crosses the locks via a cast-iron bridge with castellated abutments designed by George Stephenson. At the top of the locks is a lock cottage with a restored bridge-weight restriction plate fastened to the wall. Opposite, a warehouse with wet-dock stands forlornly in a builder's yard.

Copperas House Bridge was rebuilt from an embankment in 1990. It is the lowest on the currently restored section and has no towpath. This area has a history of printing works, and copperas is a derivative of iron sulphate used in the printing and dyeing processes.

It is hard to think of Walsden as an industrial area, but a history of iron-working goes back to mediaeval times. Textile mills, manufacture of mill equipment, printing and coal-mining have all taken place locally. Nowadays, it is a pleasant stopping-off place, with canalside pub, general stores and convenient railway station.

Navigation Notes

Between Woodhouse Bridge and Old Royd Lock, there is an obstruction in the channel near the towpath marked by four wooden posts. Pass on the non-towpath side.

There is a sanitary station at Baltimore Boats.

Todmorden Lock 19: the guillotine gate is operated by a BW Watermate Key.

Gauxholme Middle Lock 23 is to be left empty.

Copperas House Bridge is the lowest on the navigation.

Towpath Notes

Good throughout. There is no towpath through Copperas House Bridge; take care when crossing the busy main road.

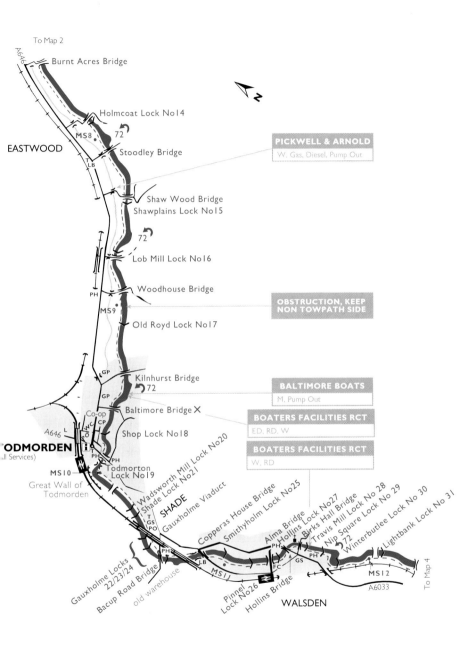

Lob Mill Lock

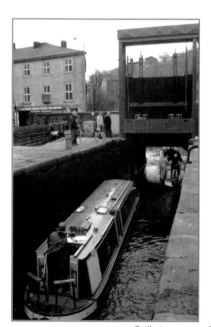

Guillotine gate at Todmorden Lock

The Great Wall of Todmorden

Shade Lock

Map 4: *Rochdale Canal*
Warland to Littleborough
3½ miles

Below Bottomley Lock an original milestone shows the distances 12½ miles to Sowerby Bridge and 19½ to Manchester.

Between the Warland Locks, the concrete box bridge was built to carry drinking water from Warland Reservoir.

A marker post next to Warland Swing Bridge marks the boundary between Yorkshire and Lancashire.

Longlees Lock marks the end of the long climb from Sowerby Bridge and the beginning of the Summit Pound. This was the first lock to be restored on the Rochdale Canal by volunteers from the Society in the seventies, with the first boats passing through at a dinghy rally on 24 August 1980. A depth gauge is mounted on the top lockgate: this is to monitor the level in Summit Pound, which was constructed to seven feet depth, so that it can act as a extra reservoir.

The canal now forms a wide weed-fringed pool passing through the spectacular scenery of the Summit Gap. The massive valley or pass is of glacial origin, being cut by melt-water during the ice age when Lancashire was flooded by a great lake. Now waterfalls cascade down the steep hillsides, flowing westwards to the River Roch and the Irish Sea, or eastwards to the Calder and the North Sea. Heather grows on the towpath, but giant pylons show their contempt for this natural beauty, electric cables spanning half a mile or so, high across the valley.

Across the fields is Steanor Bottom Toll House, still with its tariff board for the Todmorden Turnpike on display. Beyond can be seen the circular ventilation shafts and spoil heaps of the 2809-yard Summit Railway Tunnel, the scene of a spectacular fire when, in December 1984, a petrol tanker train burst into flames far down below.

West Summit Lock has a lockhouse. Above the lock the water supply from Chelburn Reservoirs enters the canal, while below the lock the derelict feeder channel from Hollingworth Lake can be seen contouring along the hillside above the canal.

Twelve locks drop the canal to Littleborough in less than two miles. From Punchbowl Locks, the railway can be seen emerging from Summit Tunnel. The valley is so narrow that there is scarcely room for canal, railway and road. The infant River Roch is forced to cross over the railway in an 'S'-shaped aqueduct. Rocky outcrops and mountains of tunnel spoil overshadow the rows of stone houses perched on narrow ledges.

During the years of the canal's closure, the factories of Fothergill & Harvey had encroached on the route. For the reopening, an office block had to be removed from over a lock chamber and a car park removed.

Where the canal crosses Lydgate Clough on a small aqueduct, the towpath has been lowered to act as a spillway, allowing surplus water to cascade into the stream. At Benthouse Lock, there is a boat dock and the base of a crane used formerly for loading stone slabs from nearby Blackstone Edge.

Dum Bridge (A58) had been infilled and has been rebuilt. At Littleborough Lock the attractive, if incongruous, 'black and white' architecture of the lock cottage is the result of adding an extra storey to the original canal company building.

Littleborough is presently the terminus of navigation, but it is a short distance through a subway beneath the railway station into this attractive, workaday little town. The Coach House Visitor Centre next to the church is run by volunteers and provides a useful insight into the town and the hills around.

Navigation Notes
Warland Swing Bridge
A drop-latch located mid-span on the upstream side locks the bridge in the closed position. Unfasten the handle using a handcuff key, lift the handle and turn at right-angles before attempting to swing the bridge.

Summit Pass Brass Plaque
As a permanent souvenir of reaching Summit Pound 600 feet above sea level, an oval brass plaque representing Longlees Lock no. 36 is available for £6 from the Rochdale Canal Society (see page 126) with proof of visit, or the lady from the lock cottage may sell you one as she did on our visit.

Winding (Turning) on Summit Pound
Full-length craft can turn just above Longlees Lock. Boats only up to 44 feet can turn above West Summit Lock.

Littleborough
Navigation may be restricted between West Summit and Littleborough — the Tuel Lane lock-keeper will advise.

Towpath Notes
Good throughout.

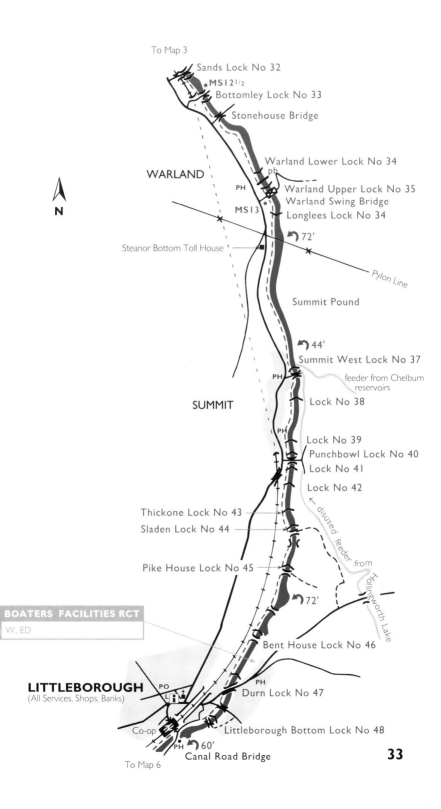

To Map 3

Sands Lock No 32

MS12¹/₂

Bottomley Lock No 33

Stonehouse Bridge

Warland Lower Lock No 34

WARLAND

pb

PH

Warland Upper Lock No 35

Warland Swing Bridge

MS13

Longlees Lock No 34

⤷ 72'

Steanor Bottom Toll House

Pylon Line

Summit Pound

⤷ 44'

Summit West Lock No 37

feeder from Chelburn reservoirs

PH

SUMMIT

Lock No 38

PH

Lock No 39

Punchbowl Lock No 40

Lock No 41

Lock No 42

Thickone Lock No 43

Sladen Lock No 44

disused feeder from

Pike House Lock No 45

⤷ 72'

Hollingworth Lake

BOATERS FACILITIES RCT

W, ED

Bent House Lock No 46

LITTLEBOROUGH
(All Services, Shops, Banks)

PO

PH

Durn Lock No 47

Co-op

Littleborough Bottom Lock No 48

PH ⤷ 60'

Canal Road Bridge

To Map 6

33

Longlees Lock

Warland

34

Longlees Lock

Map 5

Rochdale Canal Reservoirs

The Rochdale Canal Act of 1794 gave the company powers to build reservoirs on Blackstone Edge moorland and on any enclosed lands within a further 300 yards. As a condition of this, they had to supply twice as much compensation water to the rivers for use by the mills as was abstracted for the canal.

Although opened from Sowerby Bridge to Rochdale by 1798, water supply problems forced closure during 1800, the initial reservoirs proving inadequate.

Two systems of reservoirs fed the canal: the low-level Hollingworth Lake and the high-level reservoirs at over 1200 feet on Blackstone Edge.

Hollingworth Lake is lower than the Summit Pound and so a steam engine was installed around 1802 to pump water up to the feeder channel. (The canal proposals originally included a summit tunnel at a lower level which could have been fed by gravity.) The steam engine was abandoned in 1857 and the water fed directly into the canal below Littleborough.

The high-level reservoirs were finally completed in 1827, collecting water from over 2000 acres of moorland.

In 1923, all eight of the reservoirs were sold to the Rochdale and Oldham Corporations for the supply of drinking water to these growing towns. Provision was made that they must pass minimum quantities of water to the Summit Pound. In 1974, the reservoirs passed to North West Water Authority, now North West Water.

Suggested Circular Walks

Rochdale Canal Towpath up Littleborough Locks and the Summit Pound, the high-level reservoirs on Blackstone Edge and Hollingworth Lake and its canal feeder
10 miles (Map 5)

Construction of the Rochdale Canal over the Pennines resulted in a need for a vast supply of water. This walk, marked red on the map, visits the locks leading up to the summit and the reservoirs high up on Blackstone Edge, to demonstrate the enormity of the Rochdale Canal Company's water undertaking.

This walk also demonstrates how the wheel of transport has turned full circle. Early packhorse roads are seen, in turn replaced by the Rochdale Canal, The Manchester & Leeds Railway and now the M62 motorway.

The walk involves steep ascents and descents and rough tracks across high and exposed moorland. It should not be attempted in bad weather. Stout footwear and adequate clothing are required.

Start point: Littleborough Railway Station. There is adequate car parking near the station. (Boaters may wish to start their walk from Summit.)

Littleborough Railway Station stands on the Manchester & Leeds Railway, the first to cross the Pennines. Engineered by George Stephenson, it opened in competition with the Rochdale Canal in 1841, an event recorded by a stone tablet on the front of the booking office.

Pass beneath the station subway and the Rochdale Canal will be found across Canal Road. Turn left.

For a description of the towpath to Warland Swing Bridge, please turn to Map 4, page 32.

At Warland Swing Bridge, cross the bridge and follow the tarmac lane up the hill to the left of the cottages. The lane climbs the steep Warland Clough, turning sharply back right on itself in the hamlet. Notice the houses which are four-storey at the rear and two at the front. There are good views over Summit Pool.

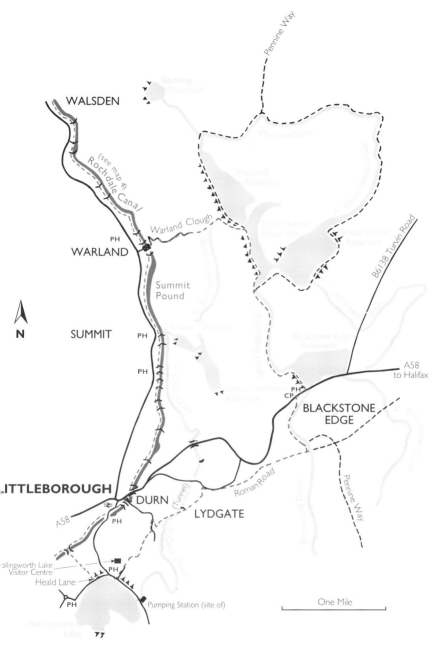

WALSDEN

Pennine Way

Gadding Reservoir

Warland Drain

(see map 4)

Rochdale Canal

Warland Reservoir

Warland Clough

Light Hazzels Reservoir

White Holme Reservoir

PH

WARLAND

B6138 Turvin Road

Summit Pound

N

SUMMIT

PH

Lower Chelburn

Blackstone Edge Reservoir

PH

A58 to Halifax

Upper Chelburn Reservoir

PH CP

BLACKSTONE EDGE

LITTLEBOROUGH

DURN

(Tunnel)

Roman Road

Pennine Way

A58

PH

LYDGATE

Hollingworth Lake Visitor Centre

Heald Lane

PH

Pumping Station (site of)

PH

One Mile

Hollingworth Lake

ROCHDALE CANAL RESERVOIRS

Hollingworth Lake	7608	lockfuls of water	Warland	3355	lockfuls of water
Blackstone Edge	2360	"	Higher Chelburn	777	"
White Holme	4944	"	Lower Chelburn	383	"
Light Hazzels	942				

37

Follow the tarmac track up through the gate. At the 'T' junction take the right-hand fork. The tarmac swings left, now becoming a muddy stoned track. Ascend slightly right in front of the derelict stone cottages through another gate and ever up the valley, keeping a boundary wall on the left.

Suddenly on the skyline ahead is the unmistakable crest of a dam. Look out for a concrete weir in the brook and a dry man-made watercourse contouring off towards Littleborough. This is Solomon's Cutting, which formerly took water down to the Chelburn Reservoirs and thus to the canal.

The track leads directly up to the gated access tunnel into the dam through a gate marked 'NWWA public footpath'. Follow the track up the right-hand flank of the dam to the crest.

This vast impounded area of water is Warland Reservoir. In front at a slightly higher level is Light Hazzles Reservoir. Follow along the crest of the dam. This well-worn path is part of the Pennine Way, Britain's first long-distance public footpath originally proposed in 1935 and opened on 24 April 1965. It runs for 250 miles from Edale in Derbyshire to Kirk Yetham across the Scottish Border.

Light Hazzles Reservoir with its elongated shape, earth embankment and 'towing path' is very reminiscent of canal construction, especially where it tapers away into a feeder channel. White Holme Reservoir can be glimpsed beyond.

As the route passes beneath the pylon line, there are extensive views across industrial Lancashire. In front, Hollingworth Lake glitters far below, while to the right the Chelburn Reservoirs creep into view.

Soon Blackstone Edge Reservoir is reached, where new work indicates considerable expense to bring this old dam up to modern safety standards.

Follow the track across the dam and turn right at the main road. The White House is an excellent place for rest and refreshment (but please note it is not open all day). Turn left on the Pennine Way (noting the roadside standing stone) and climb the path until another water feeder is reached, which should be followed right.

The purpose of Broad Head Drain is to intercept run-off water from Blackstone Edge and transfer it back to the reservoirs that have already been passed. It has been concreted by the waterworks company, but several of its older stone features remain, notably a large silt-trap with sluice to allow the silt to run away down the hillside.

At Roman Road, leave the feeder and turn right, downhill.

This ancient route has been sliced through by the canal feeder. Although probably of mediaeval rather than roman origin, this well-preserved roadway is nevertheless interesting, with its central hollow causey stones augmented on either side by paving and kerbs. The image of heavily laden carts and pack-horses on this steep incline graphically illustrates the advantages of canal transport over earlier roads. A canal boat pulled by a single horse could carry 20 times the load of a wagon, which required a team of horses, or the equivalent of 600 pack-horses.

Follow the footpath along the boundary wall, ignoring the modern A58 Halifax Road which sweeps past on the right-hand side.

At Lydgate, at the bottom of the hill, the path joins a tarmac road beyond the cottages and farm. Follow the road round the right-hand bend past the former Lydgate Mill and millpond. Immediately left, take the public footpath over the stile, marked 'South Pennine Chain'.

Take the left-hand gateway out of the far boundary of the field, then keep the stone boundary wall on your right. Keep straight on across a stile and a stream into the garden of a stone cottage and exit through the lich-gate-style gateway following the left-hand bank of the stream.

Here the derelict Hollingworth Lake feeder channel can be seen disappearing into the hillside in a tunnel to the right and contouring along the valley side ahead. The path follows it for a short while before diving down and crossing the stream, turning back on itself at a cottage and wandering down onto a tarmac road.

Turn left along the road and turn right across the small wooden bridge over the stream. This path leads to Hollingworth Lake Visitor Centre.

Hollingworth Lake Visitor Centre houses a snack bar, toilets and an exhibition of the history and function of Hollingworth Lake in supplying water to the Rochdale Canal. From the front door across the valley can be seen the feeder running toward Summit Pool. Because the lake is at a lower level, a steam pumping engine was installed on the lakeside to raise water by 45 feet, but regrettably the site is not open to the public.

Walk up to the lakeside and follow round the shore to the right.

Not only did Hollingworth Lake provide water to the canal, but it also became a well-known tourist spot. In the days of 'King Cotton' it became known as the 'Weavers' Seaport'. Today, the large expanse of water is dotted with sailing craft and canoes at weekends, their bright colours contrasting with the green and black hills all around. The whole area is managed as a country park, and perhaps the only blot on the landscape is the newest trans-Pennine route, the M62 motorway, which seems almost to cross one corner of the lake on a giant viaduct.

Follow the shoreline past the Fishermen's Inn and the reservoir valve tower. Turn right down Heald Lane. At the farm, the trackway turns into a public footpath which leaves the farmyard along the top side of the sheds. Keep the stone wall on your right, down the left side of the chemical works. Over the canal bridge, turn right on the towpath to return to Littleborough. (Note: the farmyard can get very muddy in wet weather and it may be easier to take a short cut down the road.)

This section of weed-infested waterway contrasts unfavourably with that traversed earlier. The filled-in bridge, ironically on Canal Road, is the first blockage on the restored Rochdale Canal, more than 15 miles from Sowerby Bridge.

Other Suggested Circular Walks

High Level Reservoirs
8 miles

Start from the public car park below the White House public house on the A58. Head north on the Pennine Way along the dams of Blackstone Edge, Light Hazzles and Warland Reservoirs. Then follow the Warland Drain and Whiteholme Drain round the hill to White Holme Reservoir. Then back to the regulating drain and retrace steps back to the start point.

From this route, all the Rochdale Canal reservoirs can be seen and panoramic views across Lancashire. Two windmill farms, Stoodley Pike (see page 28) and Heptonstall Church (see page 22) are also visible.

Although this walk is almost level, it crosses high, exposed and remote moorland and suitable clothing and stout footwear should be worn. Definitely a walk for a clear, warm, sunny day.

Hollingworth Lake
A variety of well-made tracks are way-marked from Hollingworth Lake Visitor Centre, and it is less than two miles to circumnavigate the lake. Users of public transport (or boaters) could start from Littleborough with a total distance less than four miles.

The walk includes the Visitor Centre with its exhibition on the reservoir and the canal, the three dams, the site of the pumping station and Summit Feeder (private land) and the Victorian tourist resort, still popular today.

Conditions can be severe in winter: Warland Reservoir

Roman road on Blackstone Edge

Hollingworth Lake

Canal Road, Littleborough: present limit of navigation from Sowerby Bridge

Map 6: *Rochdale Canal*

Littleborough to Rochdale

3¾ miles

In contrast with the steep descent into Littleborough, this is the longest level pound on the Rochdale Canal at nearly 4 miles. The valley of the River Roch widens as the high Pennine Hills are left behind.

The road to Hollingworth Lake has been straightened and the bridge filled in, bringing navigation to an end. Shortly, a chemical works stands on the far bank and here the feeder enters the canal from Hollingworth Lake.

Attractive houses front the canal at Smithy Bridge. Only the signal box remains of the original railway station; the new platforms are built on the site of the originals which were demolished in the Beeching era. It was to here that thousands of early tourists travelled to visit Hollingworth Lake from all over Lancashire.

Across Little Clegg Swing Bridge, there are some splendid examples of weavers' cottages and the village dates back to Elizabethan times.

Clegg Hall is seventeenth century. Its blackened ruin is a sad sight overlooking the canal, and it is a grade 1 listed building.

Belfield Bridge seems to mark an invisible boundary; east of here the mills are built of stone but westwards they are of brick. The canal and railway cross the River Beal on a high embankment giving impressive views across the Lancashire landscape on either side. Nearby, Belfield Hall was the home of Richard Townley JP, a major protagonist in the early scheme to employ James Brindley to design the canal in 1765.

The bridge at Milnrow has been infilled and the busy road lowered. Up through the town beyond the M62 intersection is the Ellenroad Engine House, home of the world's largest working mill steam engine, so typical of the hundreds that worked hereabouts until the 1970s. It is open Sundays (01706 881952 for a recorded message).

The approach to Rochdale is through an area of derelict mills, though many are now making way for new housing. A stub of canal between the two Moss Locks marks where an old arm led off under a bridge. A length of dry canal and an old wharf can be seen fenced off beyond the road. Below the locks, the towpath changes sides on a separate span butted up to the main road bridge.

The truncated canal arm was once a half-mile branch that led to a large basin near the town centre. Walk along Oldham Road and, just before the railway bridge, turn left up a cobbled path. Here is the restored cast-iron Halfpenny Bridge standing ignominiously among some factory units. Turn right beneath the railway bridge and the workshops of the Rochdale Canal Company are on the right, formerly canalside but now a long way from the water. Large retail establishments stand on the site of the canal basin and warehouses.

Navigation Notes

This section is not currently navigable.

Towpath Notes

Good condition throughout. At Smithy Bridge, the route makes a short diversion on an access road behind some houses, next to the signal box. On the other side of the road, there are steps down to the towpath.

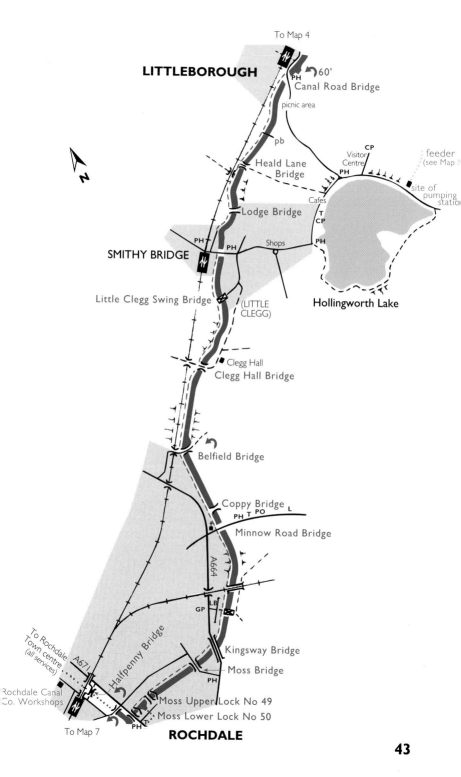

To Map 4

LITTLEBOROUGH

PH

60'

Canal Road Bridge

picnic area

pb

Heald Lane
Bridge

CP

Visitor
Centre

PH

feeder
(see Map

site of
pumping
station

Cafes

T
CP

Lodge Bridge

PH

PH

Shops

PH

SMITHY BRIDGE

Little Clegg Swing Bridge

(LITTLE
CLEGG)

Hollingworth Lake

Clegg Hall

Clegg Hall Bridge

Belfield Bridge

Coppy Bridge L

PH T PO

Minnow Road Bridge

A664

LB

GP T

To Rochdale
Town centre
(all services)

A671

Halfpenny Bridge

Kingsway Bridge

Moss Bridge

PH

Rochdale Canal
Co. Workshops

Moss Upper Lock No 49

Moss Lower Lock No 50

To Map 7

PH

ROCHDALE

43

Little Clegg

Clegg Hall

Belfield Bridge

Rochdale: Moss Locks (2)

Map 7: *Rochdale Canal*
Rochdale to Mills Hill
4½ miles

This map must contain more obstacles to canal restoration than any other in the book. Notwithstanding this, towpath improvements have been carried out and all the locks sport top gates; some are even in working condition.

As it crosses the Sudden Brook Valley, the canal has been narrowed to allow expansion of a factory — this will be a similar restoration challenge to that already carried out at Sagar Richards, Luddenden Foot (see Map 1).

Two culverted blockages once carried roads that served the Ashfield Valley housing complex: two dozen high-rise blocks with deck access which once fronted the canal. The development was a typical sixties planning failure and had to be demolished before the residents did it for themselves! Now the smart new headquarters of the Coop CRS occupy the site, turning a more friendly face to the canal.

One of the most serious blockages follows at the A627(M) Queensway Roundabout. Opened in 1971, the roundabout and two dual carriageway roads sit on the line of the canal. The agreed restoration proposals show a new channel across the roundabout and skirting the north side of the motorway. (See towpath notes below.)

The canal to Castleton is wide, deep and clear, reflecting the huge mill and tall chimney that stand alongside. At Castleton the bridge under the main road has been underfilled, and steps lead down to the towpath on the far side. There are shops and sources of refreshment nearby and the railway station is next to the canal.

Seen from Bluepits Locks, the extensive railway yards and triangular junction are used as a track maintenance yard. This is also the mainline connection of The East Lancashire Railway, a steam preservation line that operates between Heywood, Bury and Rawtenstall (0161 7647790).

Another serious blockage is the M62 motorway which crosses almost at water level. Proposals here have included diverting the canal through the nearby accommodation subway. Maden Fold Junction and a two-mile branch canal to Heywood were all swept away with the construction of the motorway.

A surprisingly rural section now takes the canal to Slattocks Top Lock 54, with its lock cottage and ivy festooning the accommodation bridge. It is a strange phenomenon that canal features everywhere seem to have at least two alternative names: this six-lock flight is no different, confusingly being known both as Laneside and Slattocks Locks.

Several of the locks hereabouts have been used as convenient structures to support large service pipes routed across the canal.

Below Scowcroft Lock, another of George Stephenson's railway bridges crosses the canal. Known locally as 'The Iron Donger', this one is in original condition and no longer in use, but has been restored and attractively repainted as a historic monument. Below here, the canal executes a horseshoe shape to enable it to cross the River Irk on a small aqueduct, rather than the massive embankment required by the railway engineers to maintain their alignment. Coneygreen and Walk Mill Locks have been restored to working order, and for some years the *Ariel* trip boat operated here from the Rose of Lancaster public house. Footpaths across the fields link the towpath with a nearby country park.

At Mills Hill, there is convenient car parking and a nearby railway station.

Navigation Notes

Portable craft may be able to use the canal at Mills Hill: contact the Rochdale Canal Trust (page 126).

Towpath Notes

Good throughout.

A627(M) Queensway Roundabout

● Heading towards Mills Hill, turn left off the towpath and follow along the same side of the dual carriageway. Cross over at the next roundabout and turn right down Gorrells Way, a minor road that passes under the motorway. Look out for the cycle lane.

● Heading towards Rochdale, turn right off the towpath under the motorway. At the end of the road, turn left; at the roundabout, cross the dual carriageway and then follow the far path down to the canal.

M62

Cross the motorway using the nearby farm-track subway. A footpath next to the houses leads back to the towpath.

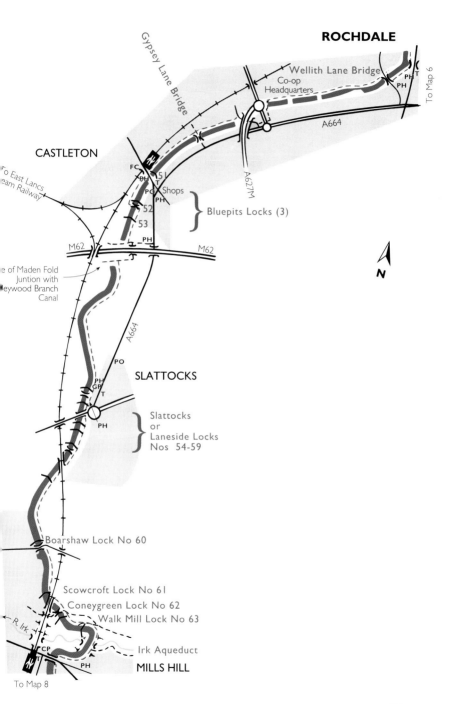

ROCHDALE

Gypsey Lane Bridge

Wellith Lane Bridge

Co-op
Headquarters

PH T
PH

To Map 6

A664

CASTLETON

To East Lancs
...eam Railway

A627M

FC
PH 51
T
PO
PH Shops

52
53

Bluepits Locks (3)

N

M62   M62

...e of Maden Fold
Juntion with
...eywood Branch
Canal

A664

PO

PH
GP
T

SLATTOCKS

PH

Slattocks
or
Laneside Locks
Nos 54-59

Boarshaw Lock No 60

Scowcroft Lock No 61
Coneygreen Lock No 62
Walk Mill Lock No 63

R. Irk

CP

PH

Irk Aqueduct

MILLS HILL

To Map 8

47

Narrowed canal at Sudden Brook

Lock used as support for pipe: Laneside Locks No. 59

Moorings at The Rose of Lancaster wait for boats

Map 8: *Rochdale Canal*
Mills Hill to Newton Heath
4¹⁄₂ miles

Leaving the Irk Valley at Mills Hill, the Rochdale Canal finally sheds the image of rurality and takes the plunge into the Manchester conurbation.

Below Kay Lane Lock, the remains of a short branch to a colliery can be seen, surprisingly built for narrow beam craft. At Foxdenton Lane, the present flat slab replaces an unusual lifting bridge. The flat deck remained horizontal and was winched up on four corner posts. Old service pipes still cross the canal at high level.

South of Foxdenton Lane, it is now difficult to imagine that the line crossed Slacks Valley on a large embankment, construction of which delayed the opening of the canal. The only clue now is the towpath-side spillweir and its cascade to the concrete-lined stream far below — the valley has almost totally disappeared with successive generations of industrial development. Now the landscape is being pushed around again for the M66 motorway and the new Chadderton Broadway industrial development.

One of the greatest successes of the Rochdale Canal Society was securing at the public inquiry a route for the canal beneath the new Manchester M66 motorway. In 1986, boats were craned in and sailed between the Boat & Horses pub and Failsworth Lock. Now the navigation has been diverted over a considerable length and sneaks beneath the road in a little concrete box. The towpath follows its own route over a footbridge.

At Failsworth, a large shopping development has been built across the canal line. Restoration proposals show a new route built through the narrowest centre section of the building.

The canal recommences beyond the shopping centre, a shallow, weed-fringed linear rubbish dump with well-groomed towpath. A large metal pipe crosses almost at water level: this is the aqueduct carrying Manchester's water supply from Thirlmere in the Lake District. Several road bridges have been lowered.

Below the three Tannersfield Locks, the infamous shallowed section commences at the Manchester City Boundary. Upstream, there are fish in the water and moorhens nest in the reeds. Downstream, the canal is a couple of inches deep and totally sterile. In 1970, the canal was filled in to just below water level

and hard-surfaced to create a safe linear park. It formed the centrepiece of the extensive council housing developments that were built on either bank. At least the route of the canal was preserved so that future restoration can take place.

There are convenient shops and pubs next to the canal at Newton Heath.

Navigation Notes

Portable craft may be able to use parts of the canal between Mills Hill and Failsworth: contact the Rochdale Canal Trust (page 126).

Towpath Notes

Oldham Road – Failsworth Shopping Centre

From Oldham Road Bridge it is possible to follow the canal line; a gap has been made in the bridge parapet and a route signposted 'Oldham Way'. However, the route is overgrown and unpleasant and leads into the loading bay area of the shops. It is preferable to turn right along Oldham Road and left through the shopping concourse. The towpath recommences near the superstore petrol filling station.

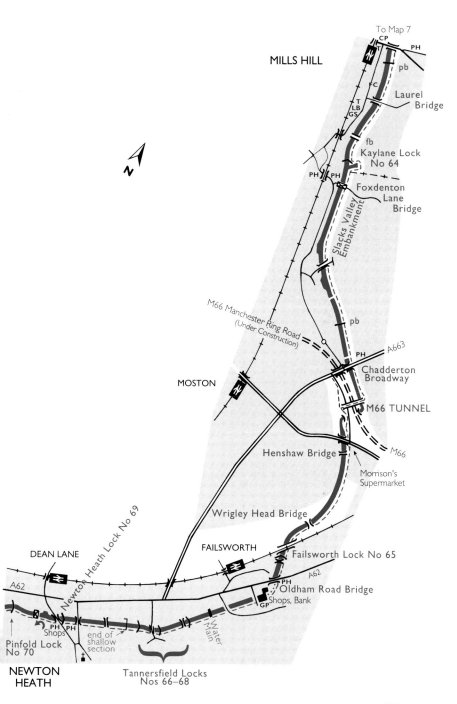

To Map 7

CP

MILLS HILL

PH

pb

FC

Laurel
Bridge

T
LB
GS

fb

Kaylane Lock
No 64

PH PH

Foxdenton
Lane
Bridge

Slacks Valley
Embankment

M66 Manchester Ring Road
(Under Construction)

pb

PH   A663

Chadderton
Broadway

MOSTON

M66 TUNNEL

Henshaw Bridge

M66

Morrison's
Supermarket

Wrigley Head Bridge

DEAN LANE

Newton Heath Lock No 69

FAILSWORTH

Failsworth Lock No 65

A62

PH

Oldham Road Bridge

A62

PH PH

Shops, Bank

GP

Shops

Water Main

Pinfold Lock
No 70

end of
shallow
section

NEWTON
HEATH

Tannersfield Locks
Nos 66–68

New tunnel built for the M66 motorway at Chadderton

The same site as above: 1986 campaign rally

Newton Heath: shallowed canal and cascaded locks

53

Map 9: *Rochdale Canal and Ashton Canal*

Central Manchester via Castlefield

5¹/₂ miles

Newton Heath to Piccadilly

A continuous flight of locks drops the canal from Newton Heath down into Manchester. At Hulme Lane the widening of the road has taken account of future restoration. Between Locks 77 and 78, the canal has not been shallowed — the factory alongside uses water from the canal and the channel acts as a reservoir. The towpath here is blocked off so a diversion is necessary (below).

At Lock 79 the huge red-brick Victoria Mill has been converted for office, retail, leisure and residential use. The travelling crane can still be seen which unloaded coal from the barges to feed the boilers in the mill basement. At Lock 80 the Navigation Inn turns its back on its waterway origins. Low-level footbridges cross the shallow channel at every opportunity.

Approaching Ancoats, industry returns. Until recently, the towpath changed sides to become part of Redhill Street and there is a separate roving bridge on the side of the road bridge. The shallowed section finishes just before the dinky cast-iron footbridge with built-in gents' urinal.

Rochdale Canal Society has done some restoration work on Ancoats and Brownsfield Locks. There is no continuous towpath between Locks 82 and 84, though Lock 83 can be visited from Tariff Street.

The huge car park area between Tariff Street and Dale Street used to be the city basins and wharves of the Rochdale Canal Company. A few warehouses still stand, the company offices are still here and cars gain access through the original arched entry.

City Centre to The Rochdale Nine

On the corner of Ducie Street and Dale Street is 111 Piccadilly, a multi-storey office block with car park formerly known as Rodwell Tower. Over the side of the car park, a canal arm and warehouse with covered boat dock can be seen. On the opposite side of Dale Street, a cobbled passage through the corner of a building leads down on to the side of Dale Street Lock 84. This lock is usually padlocked, for this is where boaters pay to use the nine locks down to Castlefield.

Lock 85 lies directly below 111 Piccadilly. Great concrete columns rise out of the canal

water giving the impression of an eerie flooded cathedral.

Trams mingle with the traffic on Aytoun Street Bridge. The towpath changes sides and becomes part of the pedestrianised Canal Street. Many of the buildings have been converted into bars, and signs proclaim this is the Gay Quarter. At Chorlton Street Lock 86, the lock-keeper's cottage sits astride the canal. At Princess Street Lock 87, a barge has been moored as a 'beer terrace', seriously obstructing passage of the lock.

At Oxford Road, the hideous backs of the buildings belie their ornate front façades. An antique cast-iron lamp standard on the lockside dates from the days when traffic proceeded both night and day.

Above Tib Lock 89, a long-lost arm was excavated and restored for narrow beam craft in 1996. It provides a water feature alongside the Bridgewater Hall which is home to the Hallé Orchestra and the BBC Philharmonic. Reflecting the music played in the concert hall, the parapets of Great Bridgewater Street Bridge are decorated in musical designs manufactured of wrought iron. The ill-fated Manchester & Salford Junction Canal used to connect to this branch (see page 63).

The canal is now dominated by giant arches holding up the former Central Station Goods Yard, before disappearing into the dark Deansgate Tunnel. High overhead, a steel and plastic tube carries pedestrians between G-Mex and Deansgate Station.

Deansgate Tunnel is in reality a long bridge, but when the canal was built this pound was a tunnel cut through solid sandstone. At the end of an arm in the pocket garden, the top of an older unlined tunnel can be seen. In 1765, when the Bridgewater Canal was opened, this tunnel led under Deansgate, where coal was lifted in boxes up a shaft to be sold on the street. When the Rochdale Canal was cut through at a higher level 35 years later, the tunnel had to be blocked off (photo page 61).

Duke's Lock, with its attractive lock cottage on one side and pub on the other, is the 92nd and last on the Rochdale Canal. The bottom gates are opened by a windlass and chain.

Castlefield is now a major tourist destination and it is worth exploring the many arms and basins of the Bridgewater Canal. Its original

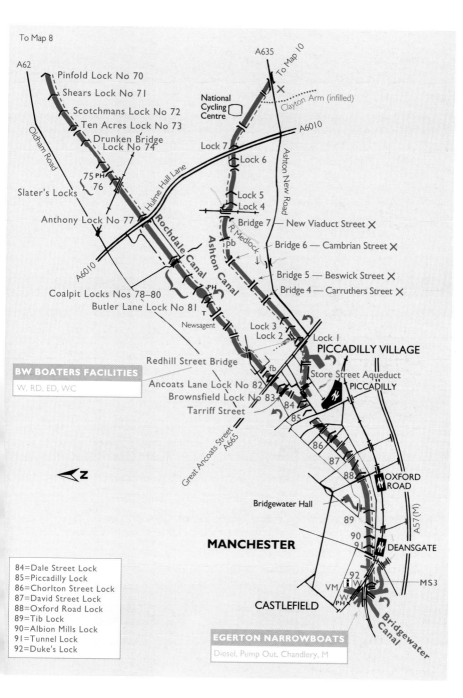

A62

Pinfold Lock No 70
Shears Lock No 71
Scotchmans Lock No 72
Ten Acres Lock No 73
Drunken Bridge
Lock No 74

75 PH
76

Slater's Locks

Anthony Lock No 77

A6010

Coalpit Locks Nos 78–80
Butler Lane Lock No 81

Newsagent

Redhill Street Bridge

Ancoats Lane Lock No 82
Brownsfield Lock No 83
Tarriff Street

Great Ancoats Street
A665

Oldham Road

Hulme Hall Lane

Rochdale Canal

Ashton Canal

PH
T

A635

To Map 10

National
Cycling
Centre

Clayton Arm (infilled)

A6010

Lock 7

Lock 6

Ashton New Road

Lock 5
Lock 4

Bridge 7 — New Viaduct Street ✕

R Medlock
pb

Bridge 6 — Cambrian Street ✕

Bridge 5 — Beswick Street ✕

Bridge 4 — Carruthers Street ✕

Lock 3
Lock 2

Lock 1

PICCADILLY VILLAGE

Store Street Aqueduct

PICCADILLY

fb

84

85

86

87

88

OXFORD
ROAD

Bridgewater Hall

89

90
91

DEANSGATE

A57(M)

92

MS3

VM

W

i

W
PH

CASTLEFIELD

MANCHESTER

Bridgewater
Canal

✕ Z

84 = Dale Street Lock
85 = Piccadilly Lock
86 = Chorlton Street Lock
87 = David Street Lock
88 = Oxford Road Lock
89 = Tib Lock
90 = Albion Mills Lock
91 = Tunnel Lock
92 = Duke's Lock

EGERTON NARROWBOATS

Diesel, Pump Out, Chandlery, M

terminus is round to the left on an arm that was once part of the River Medlock. The Grocer's Warehouse shows how water power was used to lift goods from the boats. Old wharves and warehouses are continually being restored and put to new uses. But it was not always so: in 1988, when the Inland Waterways Association National Waterways Festival was held here, most of the area was derelict and some of the arms filled in.

From Duke's Lock follow round to the right beneath the towering railway viaducts. The twin arms in the shape of a tuning fork once led into the Staffordshire Warehouse and are now visitor moorings. At the top of the steps is the Castlefield Visitor Centre with tourist information and interpretation of the canal scene.

This is the best place from which to explore central Manchester. Across the road is the original Liverpool Road Station of Stephenson's *Rocket* fame, now part of the Manchester Museum of Science & Industry. Up the road are the remains of the Roman castle which gave the area its name. Round the corner is Granada Studio Tours. And Manchester's main shopping area is only half a mile away up Deansgate.

Ashton Canal: Piccadilly to Clayton

For boaters, entering the narrow Ashton after the wide bridges and locks of the Rochdale is something of a shock. On the right, a huge railway warehouse stands on the site of the canal's original city terminal basins which once stretched as far as London Road.

Pedestrians approach the towpath from Ducie Street down a stone cart track. Paradise Wharf warehouse is a night club, overlooking the Claymore, a floating restaurant cafe bar. This Leeds & Liverpool barge has been fitted with a square superstructure making it look like a large floating box!

Store Street is crossed on a mellow stone aqueduct, its angled pedestrian refuges reminiscent of a mediaeval river bridge. Piccadilly Village follows, a complex of modern housing built around the basins of Meadow Street Wharves.

When trade was at its busiest, a start was made on duplicating the locks. Only Locks 1, 17 and 18 were completed, and here the bywash is now routed through the redundant chamber. Locks 1 and 2 have mitred double top gates, unusual on a narrow canal.

The towpath crosses the truncated Islington branch and a group of canal buildings. Dennis Howell, then Labour Minister for Sport, unveiled a plaque here in 1974 celebrating the reopening of the canals back up to Marple.

Above the locks the route starts as a dreary canyon between decaying factories punctuated by low bridges, before passing huge (and nowadays rare) gas-holders. Bridge 7, New Viaduct Street, is an aqueduct over the River Medlock with both road and rail bridges over the top.

At Lock 7 the towpath changes sides. The steep cobbled towpath crossover bridge facing the canal must have been very dangerous for boat horses, especially on an icy morning. Next to the canal and dominating the view is the new indoor National Cycling Centre, the huge dome looking frighteningly like an alien spacecraft from the movie *Independence Day*.

Navigation Notes

Rochdale Canal

A separate licence must be purchased from the Rochdale Canal Company to navigate the nine locks (details 0161 236 2456). You are recommended to check opening hours, etc. in advance. Access to the head of Locks 86 and 87 is difficult due to lack of landings and, if sufficient crew are available, it would be ideal to send them on ahead.

Turn sharp right at the top of the locks for the Ashton Canal: there is no navigation between Piccadilly and Failsworth.

Ashton Canal

All paddle gear at locks is fitted with handcuff key locks. This area has an unenviable reputation for vandalism. Do not leave a boat unattended and keep the front doors locked. Ideally, set off early in the morning and avoid school holidays where possible. British Waterways can sometimes provide an escort service through the locks (0161 427 1079).

Towpath Notes

Rochdale Canal

Between Locks 77 and 78, the towpath is closed. Diversions can be made on roads parallel to the canal at either side.

There is no continuous towpath between Locks 82 (Great Ancoats Street) and 84 (Dale Street). Divert on the south side via Laystall Street and Ducie Street.

Lock 85 is situated in a long underground section which can be intimidating. If in doubt, divert along Ducie Street and across London Road.

Ashton Canal

Access to the towpath is from Ducie Street.

National Cycling Centre

Ashton Canal

Gasworks

Lock 3, Ashton Canal

Locks 1 and 2, Ashton Canal, with their unusual double top-gates

Piccadilly Village, Ashton Canal

Rochdale Canal: Dukes Lock No. 92

59

Entry to the Rochdale Canal basins from Dale St

Lock 82

Rochdale Canal

National Waterways Festival 1988, Deansgate

Old Bridgewater Canal Tunnel at Deansgate (see page 54)

Bridgewater Hall

Castlefield: Grocers' Warehouse

Waterways World

the *NUMBER ONE* inland waterway magazine

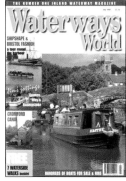

● **enjoy the waterways –** explore different canals and rivers each month with cruising reports, waterside walks, hire boat reviews, continental cruising

● **discover canal heritage** in waterway histories that tell of the boats, people and companies that built and worked the canal system

● **follow waterway news** with reports that tell you all that is happening on canals and rivers

● **get afloat –** *Waterways World* has more canal boats for sale and hire than any other magazine

● **practical advice** for boat owners and aspiring boat owners – new and used boat reviews, engine developments, the latest equipment, and much more

●

Available from newsagents, boatyards and on subscription

Published by Waterways World Ltd, The Well House, High Street, Burton-on-Trent, Staffordshire DE14 1JQ. Telephone (01283) 742950 Fax (01283) 742966

History of the Manchester & Salford Junction Canal

From 1806, there were two unconnected waterway systems serving Manchester:

1. The Manchester, Bolton & Bury Canal was linked to the River Irwell and thus the Mersey.
2. The Bridgewater Canal was linked to the Rochdale and Ashton Canals and via the Trent & Mersey and Leeds & Liverpool Canals, to the rest of the country.

The Mersey & Irwell Navigation looked jealously at all the traffic coming from the Rochdale and Ashton Canals and going onto the Bridgewater.

The Bolton & Bury wanted connections with other lines: at that time goods for destinations around the country had first to be transhipped by carts.

Their answer was the Manchester & Salford Junction Canal. Opened in 1838, it descended from the Rochdale Canal across the site of Bridgewater Hall through four locks to the Irwell where the bottom lock can be seen in the Granada Studio Tours site. Most of the half-mile route was in tunnel and it was expensive to operate as the Rochdale Company would not let the newcomer have any water, so it had all to be backpumped up the flight.

Seeing the challenge, the Bridgewater opened its own connection with the Irwell in the same year at Hulme Locks, just below Castlefield. These served the same purpose at less cost.

The M&SJC struggled on until 1875 when part was filled in for the new Central Railway Station (now G-Mex). The tunnel was last used as an air-raid shelter in the Second World War, though, as it still exists beneath Granada Studio Tours, who knows what its future might be?

The Ashton Canal System at its Peak

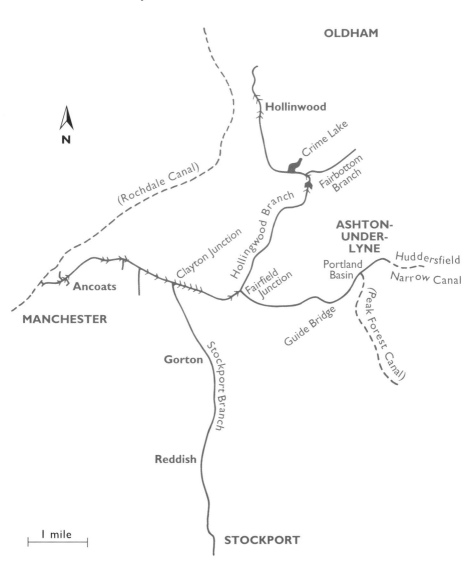

History of the Ashton Canal

Until the coming of the Duke of Bridgewater's Canal, Manchester's coal had traditionally been supplied in the Oldham–Ashton–Hyde area. In order to compete with the Worsley mines, a canal was needed. In 1792, parliamentary approval was given for canals from Manchester Piccadilly to Ashton and Oldham, and an Act in the following year gave authority for a line to Stockport. Carrying commenced in 1797.

At the same time, the Peak Forest Canal was being constructed to open up the limestone trade from high up in the Peak District. This connected near the Ashton terminus, further extending this network of narrow canals.

From inception, the Ashton and Peak Forest worked closely together. From 1803, they shared a joint management team. Trade was very successful, and continued to increase with the opening of the Huddersfield Narrow Canal and the High Peak Railway (a horse-drawn tramway), linking across the Peak District to the Cromford Canal and the Trent. In 1831, the network expanded further with the opening of the Macclesfield Canal, giving Manchester a shorter water route to Stoke-on-Trent and London.

By 1847, the Ashton, Peak Forest and Macclesfield Canals were in the ownership of the Manchester, Sheffield & Lincolnshire Railway, passing via the Great Central and London & North Eastern Railways to state ownership. By the mid-1950s trade had ceased. British Transport Commission closed the Hollinwood Branch from Fairfield Junction in 1955 and the Stockport Branch was filled in in 1962. However, the Macclesfield Canal and the Peak Forest above Marple had become popular for the new hobby of pleasure boating.

At this time, officialdom discouraged pleasure boaters from the Ashton and the Peak Forest below Marple, and the canals rapidly became unnavigable. The closure became official when part of Marple aqueduct collapsed in 1962.

Failure of this historic monument was the turning point. Waterways enthusiasts and the local councils raised the additional cost of repair over demolition. Boat rallies were held, and work parties cleared the channel and locks, culminating in two mighty 'Big-Digs' with over 1000 volunteer 'navvies' at each. British Waterways agreed to restore the two canals with funding from the local authorities, and the reopening finally took place in 1974.

The Ashton, Peak Forest, and Macclesfield Canals — together with the Trent & Mersey, Bridgewater, and Rochdale — now form a circular cruising route, the 'Cheshire Ring', popular especially with hire boaters and making for an energetic week's holiday. The volunteer navvies continue as Waterway Recovery Group, a national organisation assisting in waterway restoration throughout the country.

Restoration Works in Progress

Moderna Bridge, Rochdale Canal (see also page 25)

Copperas Bridge, Walsden, Rochdale Canal, built 1990

Making lockgates at the Rochdale Canal Trust Callis Mill Workshops: these gates are for the Chesterfield Canal (see advertisement page 76)

Huddersfield Narrow Canal at Brownhill Bridge, Saddleworth (contrast with page 84)

Map 10: *Ashton Canal*

Clayton to Guide Bridge

3½ miles

Eleven further locks in 1½ miles lift the canal to the Ashton level. The route is lined with factories and fishermen and there seems to be a pub at every bridge. Between Locks 10 and 11, a short spur beneath a towpath bridge is all that is left of the line to Stockport. At Lock 13, the swing bridge that used to cross the lock chamber has been removed. Looking downhill, there are views across Manchester city centre.

Above Lock 16, the industry is gradually replaced by housing. Two swing bridges make a change from the continuing procession of locks and between, on the towpath, is a rare concrete BTC (British Transport Commission) boundary post.

A number of interesting features are centred on the Top Lock 18, where British Waterways keep the lockside in pristine condition. Below is a boathouse dated 1833 which was built to house a packet boat. The lock has been duplicated (as has Lock 17 below). A single-span bridge allows unobstructed use of the towrope in the further lock chamber. Distinctive steps lead up onto the lock island. There is a lock-keeper's cabin on the lockside. Everything is built from an attractive mellow stone.

Immediately above is Fairfield Junction and the stub remains of the Hollinwood Branch which ran northwards 2½ miles to Waterhouses. Here were four locks, the middle pair being a staircase. Above, the canal split into two further branches and came within a few hundred yards of the Rochdale Canal at Failsworth. Pleasure steamers took Victorian passengers along the canal to Crime Lake, a large area of water accidentally impounded by the canal when a culvert beneath an embankment failed. Today Crime Lake and the remains of the locks can be explored as they form part of the Daisy Nook Country Park managed by Oldham Borough Council (Visitor Centre 0161 620 8202).

At Bridge 17 the buildings on Fieldings Wharf are now converted to housing. Bridge 18 is more modern, but has towrope rollers and an 81 number plate fixed upside-down!

Through Audenshaw the suburbs are more attractive, with parkland in evidence and expensive-looking houses backing down to the canal. The new M66 Manchester Ring Road is

under construction across the canal between Bridges 24 and 25. Beyond, there are moored boats at Victorian Boatyard. A 2 ft-gauge railway is being built incorporating full-size artefacts, and a rudimentary side slipway into the canal features similar equipment.

The canal approaches Guide Bridge in a deep cutting. Access to the station and shops here is up steps to the Boundary public house car park. Ashton Packet Boat Co. operate the horse-drawn trip boat *Maria* from Guide Bridge

Navigation Notes

All paddle gear at locks is fitted with handcuff key locks. This area has an unenviable reputation for vandalism. Do not leave a boat unattended and keep the front doors locked. Ideally, set off early in the morning and avoid school holidays where possible. British Waterways can sometimes provide an escort service through the locks (tel 0161 427 1079).

Look out for the horse-drawn trip boat — remember, it cannot stop. Always pass on the side away from the towpath,

Towpath Notes

Good throughout.

Lock 8

To Map 9

PH

Lock 9

pb

Lock 10

Stockport Branch
(infilled)

Lock 11

Clayton Junction

Lock 12

CLAYTON

Lock 13

PH

A662

Lock 14

Lock 15

OPENSHAW

PH

Lock 16

PH

A635

Swing bridge

Swing bridge

PH

Lock 17
old boathouse

16

Fairfield
Junction

Lock 18

Hollinwood Branch
(infilled)

Fielding's
Wharf

17

FAIRFIELD

18

PH

DROYLSDEN

19

20

M66 (Under Construction)

21

24

M66

25

PH

26

PH

GUIDE BRIDGE

Shops

To Map 11

69

Clayton Junction: the Stockport Branch was on the left

Ashton Canal

Duplicated Lock 18 at Fairfield Junction

Portland Warehouse: rebuilt 1998

Map 11: *Ashton Canal and Huddersfield Narrow Canal*

Ashton and Stalybridge

4 miles

Portland Basin is the junction with the Peak Forest Canal. This is an interesting place to visit, dominated on one side by Portland Warehouse and all round by mills and mill chimneys. The Peak Forest departs beneath an elegant stone horse bridge, immediately crossing over the River Tame on a robust aqueduct. Once a year the scene is animated by Tameside Canals Festival, a major boat rally organised by the Huddersfield Canal Society. For the rest of the year they operate their trip boat *Greater Manchester* here. From Portland Basin it is a half-mile walk into Ashton town centre with its extensive pedestrianised shopping area.

Portland Warehouse burned down in 1972. At the time of writing, it is being rebuilt back to its original appearance as the centrepiece of a £7.1 million Single Regeneration Budget Scheme. The new development is intended to include an industrial museum and a cafe.

The imposing Cavendish Mill has been converted into flats. Beyond Cavendish Bridge a giant Asda superstore has been built over the canal, creating a long new tunnel without a towpath. Stop before the tunnel for shopping and refilling the petrol tank.

Whitelands Bridge and Lock 1W mark the start of the Huddersfield Narrow Canal. Because of bridge-widening at Locks 1W and 2W, the bottom gates do not have balance beams and are operated by hydraulic rams. (There is a unique numbering system on the Huddersfield Narrow Canal: locks to the west of Standedge Tunnel have a 'W' suffix and those to the east an 'E'.)

The long narrow section above Lock 1W is known as Whitelands Tunnel and has been opened out as three short bridges — the top one shows how the tunnel probably looked originally.

The route from Ashton to Stalybridge is industrial all the way. The canal crosses the River Tame at Stalybridge aqueduct. The original structure collapsed and was replaced by the present one in 1875. It is unusual in being two structures with a gap between: a cast-iron water channel and a stone towpath bridge. Milestone 19 is in the parapet and rollers on the edge suggest that there are drain plugs in the bottom of the canal which could be used

to let the water out: a feature of all the Huddersfield Narrow aqueducts.

Staley Wharf is the current head of navigation. The whole area, including Bayley Street Bridge, had been filled in and has been re-excavated. The reopening was well and truly celebrated by 'The Staley Wharf Golden Rally of Boats 1947–97', held Spring Bank Holiday 1997 to commemorate that it was fifty years since boats had last traded here. Staley Wharf has canalside pub and fish and chips, nearby petrol filling station and is convenient for town-centre shopping.

The canal through Stalybridge and three locks were filled in around 1970. The first lock was alongside the petrol station, the second beneath the Castle Hill Sports & Leisure Centre and the third upstream of Trinity Street. Early restoration proposals were for a diversion along the River Tame but, with the closure of the large factory between Trinity Street and Mottram Road, the canal will now be restored along its original line, although some modifications are necessary to cope with recent town-centre developments and two buildings will be partly demolished. Part of the original route can still be seen where it crosses Melbourne Street as a footpath. Lock 6W will be re-sited in the middle of Armentières Square.

At Mottram Road the canal re-emerges at Lock 7W and alongside there are the remains of an old crane base. Emerging from Knowl Bridge, there is a transformation: for the first time since Manchester, the canal throws off its industrial image, contouring along the side of a green valley with views ahead of the high Pennine hills. Parallel to the canal an old railway line has been converted into a bridlepath, 'The Staley Way', ideal for circular walks with the towpath.

By Lock 8W, a national grid pylon straddles the canal. This was the site of Hartshead Power Station where a quarter of a mile of infilled canal has been rebuilt.

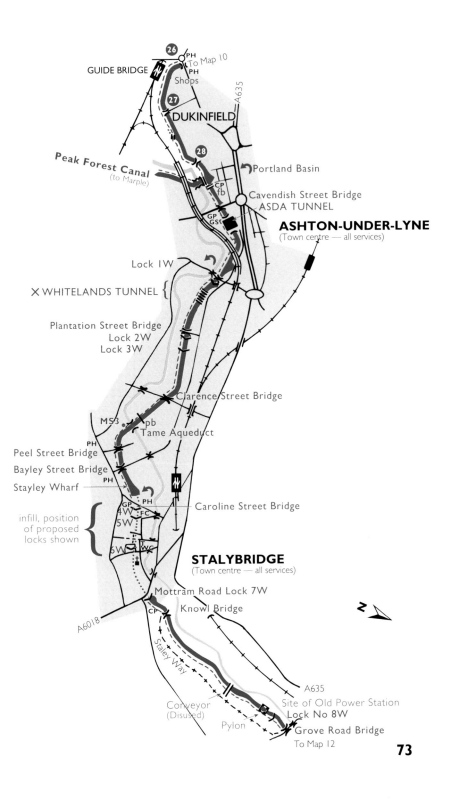

26
PH
To Map 10
PH
GUIDE BRIDGE
Shops

27
DUKINFIELD

A635

28
Portland Basin

CP
fb
Cavendish Street Bridge
ASDA TUNNEL

GP
GS

ASHTON-UNDER-LYNE
(Town centre — all services)

Lock 1W

X WHITELANDS TUNNEL {

Plantation Street Bridge
Lock 2W
Lock 3W

Clarence Street Bridge

MS3   pb
Tame Aqueduct

PH
Peel Street Bridge
Bayley Street Bridge
PH
Stayley Wharf

GP   PH
infill, position   4W   FC   Caroline Street Bridge
of proposed   5W
locks shown
6W   WC

STALYBRIDGE
(Town centre — all services)

Mottram Road Lock 7W
CP   Knowl Bridge

A6018

Staley Way

A635
Site of Old Power Station
Lock No 8W

Conveyor
(Disused)

Pylon   Grove Road Bridge
To Map 12

Peak Forest Canal
(to Marple)

73

Navigation Notes

The bottom gates of Locks 1W and 2W are not fitted with balance beams. Paddles and gates are operated by hydraulic pumps mounted on the lockside using a normal windlass. Security locks are released with a handcuff key.

A horse-drawn trip boat operates in this area — see note on page 68.

Towpath Notes

Asda Tunnel

Follow the towpath diversion straight ahead along the south side of the building. A path and steps alongside the railway viaduct lead down to the towpath.

Stalybridge

Turn left along the front of the petrol filling station and first right into Castle Street, passing the Castle Hill Sports & Leisure Centre. Turn right into the public car park area, and left on a footpath between buildings, which is clearly on the line of the canal. Cross over Melbourne Street into Armentières Square. Turn diagonally left across the square and turn into Corporation Street which is on the left side of Holy Trinity & Christ Church. At the end of Corporation Street turn right up the hill — the canal will be found by the traffic lights.

Asda Tunnel

Whitelands 'Tunnel'

74

Lock 7W, Mottram Road

Staley Wharf

75

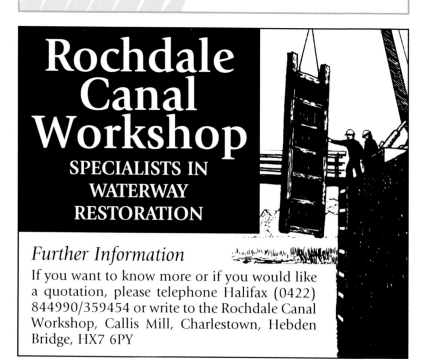

History of the Huddersfield Narrow Canal

It seemed like a good idea to build a new navigation from the Ashton Canal to Sir John Ramsden's Huddersfield Broad Canal, thus providing the shortest route over the Pennines. The Engineer, Benjamin Outram, reported that it could be built in five years, so in 1794 parliamentary approval was obtained and work started immediately from either end.

Building the Canal

Things went well enough in the Tame and Colne Valleys for, by 1799, the canal was completed from Ashton up to Woolroad and from Marsden down to Huddersfield. But to penetrate through the Pennine hills meant building a tunnel over three miles long beneath Standedge Moor. Work in the tunnel had run into serious difficulties, both engineering and financial. The company started to transfer goods over Standedge by pack-horse.

The tunnel took over 16 years to complete, through navigation commenced in April 1811. The tunnel alone had cost more than the estimates for the entire canal. It is almost $3\frac{1}{4}$ miles long, has three passing places but no towpath, and took the leggers up to $3\frac{1}{2}$ hours to work the boats through. (Leggers were gangs of men specifically employed to work the boat though the tunnel: they lay on their backs on the boat and worked it through by 'walking' against the tunnel sides or roof.) The tunnel passes through hard sandstone and grit and a considerable length is unlined.

The problems were not over. The Huddersfield Narrow, like the Ashton to which it connected, was built with narrow locks 70 feet long. However, Sir John Ramsden's Canal and the Calder & Hebble Navigations had Yorkshire-size broad locks, capable of admitting a barge only 57 feet long. Thus narrow boats could not pass beyond Huddersfield, and through cargoes had to be transhipped. Also, trade did not reach anticipated levels and the company only managed occasionally to pay a small dividend after the first in 1824.

Railways

By 1844 a railway was proposed between Leeds, Huddersfield and Manchester and this company agreed to purchase the canal. The purchase was of great benefit to them in the building of their line, especially in boring the first single-line railway tunnel. Cross-tunnels were built from the canal tunnel and spoil was shipped out from the construction work by narrow boat.

A second single-line railway tunnel was built in 1871, and the twin-track tunnel in use today was added in 1894. By this time, there was little trade left using the canal tunnel. The canal was abandoned by an Act of 1944, but the channel continued to supply water for industrial use.

Revivals

The last boat to pass through the entire canal was the *Ailsa Craig* in 1948, on hire to the infant Inland Waterways Association who were campaigning for the canal's retention. It is possible this had the opposite effect, for the passage of the boat through the derelict canal caused many interruptions to various industrial water supplies and the British Transport Commission quickly removed lockgates to prevent further such voyages.

The Huddersfield Canal Society was founded in 1974 and has been very successful in promoting restoration of the canal. Most of the locks have been repaired, much of the canal dredged, and navigation returned to Stalybridge. Now attention centres once more on Standedge Tunnel and serious blockages in Stalybridge, Slaithwaite and Huddersfield. Formation of a partnership between the Society, British Waterways and the local authorities, and the award of a millennium grant, means that through navigation should once more be possible in the new century.

Map 12: *Huddersfield Narrow Canal*
Mossley to Greenfield
3¹/₂ miles

Grove Road Bridge is a new structure replacing a flattened swing bridge. The rails on which the old bridge swung can still be seen on the canal bank (see photo, page 9).

The valley now becomes much narrower and wooded and the locks more frequent as the canal makes its assault on the summit. A narrow bank separates river from canal. All the locks on this section have been restored.

Scout Tunnel, 205 yards long, has a towpath, but this is presently blocked off and a path leads over the top. The tunnel bores through a rocky bluff in a particularly narrow section of the valley. In wet weather, it is worth walking onto the footbridge over the river to see the white-water rapids below.

Above the tunnel steps lead up from the river. This is the finish of the Tameside Canoe Trail which starts at the car park by The Roaches pub at Lock 15W. Canoeists can enjoy the flow of the river coming downstream (including some weirs) before returning on the still waters of the canal.

Between the tunnel and Lock 12W, the whole valley side had slipped towards the river, taking the canal and a disused railway embankment with it. Major stabilisation works have been carried out so that this short length of canal could be restored. Above Lock 12W the canal is a wide regular sweep of water in a wooded cutting.

Passing through Mossley the landscape is dominated by the grey-stone architecture of the town and the church spire, all terraced up the impossibly steep-looking side of the valley. In the valley bottom, mills and factories are interspersed with riverside fields, recreation grounds and woodland. Both The Roaches and The Tollemache Arms are next to the canal between Locks 15W and 16W.

The valley widens and the canal crosses the Tame again on Royal George Aqueduct, a two-span structure. Royal George Mill, the extensive mill dam and the associated cottages are alongside Lock 19W. Both Mann's Wharf Bridge and Frenche's Bridge had been filled in for road improvements and both are now reopened.

Navigation Notes
Not currently navigated.

Towpath Notes
Note that above Scout Tunnel and Lock 12W, the towpath is on the right-hand side looking upstream.

Note that the towpath changes sides at Lock 14W.

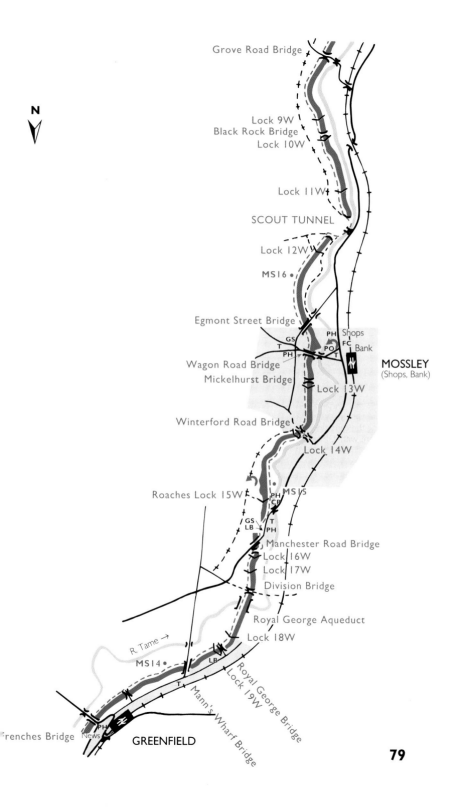

N

Grove Road Bridge

Lock 9W
Black Rock Bridge
Lock 10W

Lock 11W

SCOUT TUNNEL

Lock 12W

MS16 •

Egmont Street Bridge

GS
T
PH

PH Shops
PO
FC Bank
T

MOSSLEY
(Shops, Bank)

Wagon Road Bridge
Mickelhurst Bridge

Lock 13W

Winterford Road Bridge

Lock 14W

Roaches Lock 15W

MS15
PH
CB
T

GS
LB
PH

Manchester Road Bridge
Lock 16W
Lock 17W

Division Bridge

Royal George Aqueduct

Lock 18W

R. Tame →

MS14 •

LB

T

Lock 19W

Royal George Bridge

Mann's Wharf Bridge

Frenches Bridge   News

GREENFIELD

79

Scout Tunnel and Lock 12W

Royal George Aqueduct

Uppermill: stepping stones connect the towpath with the park.

Saddleworth Viaduct and Brownhill Visitor Centre

Map 13: *Huddersfield Narrow Canal*

Greenfield to Diggle

$3^1/_2$ miles

Frenche's Bridge is a new stone-faced concrete structure, as it had been previously embanked. At Halls Lock there are rope marks on top of the bridge parapet. Above, the towpath is squeezed between canal and river, with wooded slopes on one hand and playing fields on the other.

The 13 milestone is in the wall below Wade Lock. Above, the towpath changes sides. Uppermill is an attractive little town with quaint stone architecture. It has become a popular tourist venue with cafes, antique, craft and book shops. Saddleworth Museum and Tourist Information Centre is the start point for the *Pennine Moonraker* trip boat. This was the first section of the Huddersfield Narrow to be restored, and rejuvenation of the canal and town have gone hand in hand. This section is the venue of the annual 'Saddleworth Canals Festival' organised by the Huddersfield Canal Society.

The towpath changes sides at Moorgate Bridge. Stepping stones cross the River Tame to St Chad's playing fields. Dungebooth and Lime Kiln Locks were restored by volunteers of the Huddersfield Canal Society. Saddleworth Railway Viaduct, tall, slender and curved, dominates the scene. Beneath is Old Sag Aqueduct and it is worth viewing from the river bank to see why it got its name. The roller on the canal edge was used when pulling a plug in the canal bed, allowing the water to drain directly into the river below.

Brownhill Visitor Centre has changing exhibitions on local and wildlife scenes, together with a small bookshop and public toilets. Across the canal a wildlife park and picnic area have been constructed. The narrow concrete channel at Brownhill Bridge was opened in 1987; previously the canal had been infilled as part of a road-widening scheme.

The slipway is on the site of a large stone warehouse with covered dock similar to that at Marsden. Opposite is the wooden cantilevered transhipment warehouse now used as a meeting room. Before Standedge Tunnel was completed, cargoes were unloaded here and transferred to pack-horses for the journey over to Marsden.

At Woolroad the scenery changes with views of the high Pennine hills ahead. Heather grows on the towpath and canal banks. The nine locks of the Diggle Flight were built later than the others on the canal in time for the opening of Standedge Tunnel and have unique features. The flight was built to speed the passage of boats by giving an unobstructed route for the towing line. Single top and bottom gates and all paddle gear are mounted on the further bank and could quickly be operated by one boatman.

Above Lock 28W, look out for the mysterious, curved, dark, dank pedestrian subway beneath the canal.

Above Ward Lane Bridge, the path on the bank furthest from the railway is in better condition. Locks 31W and 32W were restored by Society volunteers.

The canal crosses high over Diggle Brook on an embankment, before plunging into the pitch-black end of Standedge Tunnel. The date '1893' on the portal indicates that the canal tunnel was extended with the building of the double track rail tunnel. Indeed, the canal used to sweep further up the Diggle Brook Valley. By crossing over the railway bridge and walking to the bus turning circle, it is possible to see a short length of original canal channel and the original Diggle Brook Aqueduct.

At 650 feet above sea level, Standedge Tunnel is the highest point on the British canal system.

Navigation Notes

Trailboats licensed for British Waterways can use the slipway at Brownhill Visitor Centre car park free of charge. The slipway is locked and the key is kept at the Visitor Centre (01457 872598). Telephone in advance before visiting.

Towpath Notes

Good walking throughout; between Ward Lane and Standedge Tunnel the path on the side furthest from the railway is easier walking.

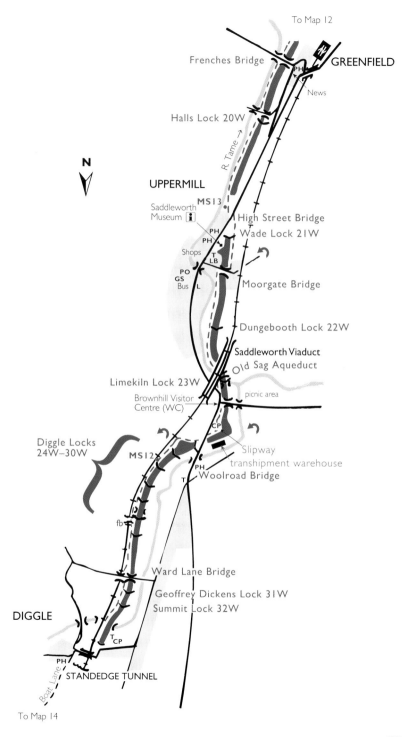

To Map 12

Frenches Bridge

GREENFIELD

PH

News

Halls Lock 20W

R. Tame

N

UPPERMILL

MS13

Saddleworth
Museum ℹ

High Street Bridge

PH
PH

Wade Lock 21W

Shops

T
LB

PO
GS
Bus   L

Moorgate Bridge

Dungebooth Lock 22W

Saddleworth Viaduct
Old Sag Aqueduct

Limekiln Lock 23W

picnic area

Brownhill Visitor
Centre (WC)

CP

Diggle Locks
24W–30W

MS12

Slipway
transhipment warehouse

PH

T

Woolroad Bridge

fb

Ward Lane Bridge

Geoffrey Dickens Lock 31W
Summit Lock 32W

DIGGLE

T
CP

PH

Boat Lane

STANDEDGE TUNNEL

To Map 14

83

Narrow concrete channel at Brownhill Bridge (see also page 67)

Woolroad Transhipment Warehouse

Diggle Locks

Diggle: short length of disconnected canal by the bus turning circle

85

Map 14: *Huddersfield Narrow Canal*
Standedge Tunnel, Diggle to Marsden
4 miles

(Text includes directions when walking from Diggle to Marsden. See below for alternative instructions when heading from Marsden to Diggle.)

The walk over Standedge Tunnel involves steep ascents and descents and rough tracks across high and exposed moorland. It should not be attempted in bad weather. Stout footwear and adequate clothing are required. In bad weather, consider catching the train from Greenfield to Marsden or the bus from Woolroad to Marsden. (Public transport, see page 122.)

Boat Lane is signposted, a gravel track between stone walls commencing on the left-hand side of the Diggle Hotel. [A] On the left, the railway is in a deep cutting supported by retaining walls as it approaches the tunnel.

Three railway tunnels can be seen: The original single-track one is in the centre with the second 1871 tunnel nearest, and both these are disused. The present railway lines describe a gentle 'S'-bend as they cross over the extended canal tunnel, to enter the 1894-built double-track bore. Between the tunnel entrances, a water tank can be seen which formerly fed railway water troughs. These allowed steam engines to take water on the move and were placed in a level section of track between the rails. The only level section on this railway was the inside of the tunnel.

Follow the track up the hill. Spoil heaps from the tunnels can be seen across the fields on the left. At a row of houses [B], ignore the tarmac track as it swings to the left — carry straight on uphill though the gate on the rough track marked 'bridleway' and 'Oldham Way', keeping the stone wall on the left.

Soon, further spoil heaps are reached and the track twists and turns at their very foot. Follow left round the top of the spoil heaps, in front of a solitary cottage [C], which is derelict at the time of writing. The capped Brun Clough shaft can be seen and a little further on there is a masonry circle: this is a further shaft attempted for the double-track rail line, but abandoned due to flooding.

In front and above, a dam can be seen with a gateway at the left-hand end. Leave the track on a bend, following the footpath diagonally up the hillside to the gate [D]. Brun Clough is

a canal reservoir and is 600 feet directly over the tunnel.

Walk between reservoir and main road, crossing a car park and joining the Pennine Way heading towards Edale. The path climbs up on the side of Standedge Cutting, paralleling the A62 before veering right through a gate.

An unmistakable wide grassy road curves gently round the contour, with Redbrook Reservoir and its sailing club away down to the left. Once upon a time this track was the main road over Standedge, a turnpike built in the 1780s. After a short distance, a stream has washed out the turnpike [E]. There is a paved diversion on the reservoir side, while the Pennine Way veers away southwards.

It is not entirely clear which route the Boat Lane followed down to Marsden. It probably skirted round Redbrook Reservoir and paralleled the A62 (which was built later). While the tunnel was being built, goods had to be carted between Woolroad and Marsden. Once complete, in the busy carrying days of this canal, I cannot imagine the cosy picture of the boat horse being led over the tunnel while the boat was legged through. I would surmise (with no evidence, because it is before living memory) that horses would be changed at the end of the tunnel and work back the way they had come with a different boat. (Horses would be too valuable a piece of equipment to spend half a day strolling over the hillside, and in the winter it might be impassable.) Hence the Boat Lane would become unused and lost. I have chosen to follow the old turnpike which is contemporary with the canal but also keeps away from the noisy traffic on the A62.

Beyond Redbrook Reservoir is the conical shaped Pule Hill, bearing the scars of more tunnel shafts and also extensive stone quarries.

Over a rise, a water channel crosses the turnpike, its stone lining leading down the hillside on the right and contouring away to the left. This was a canal company leat, linking Black Moss and Swellands Reservoirs to Redbrook Reservoir.

A wooden post marks where the turnpike has been washed away by another stream [F]. Scramble down the bank, across the plank bridge to the tarmac road opposite. Cross over onto Old Mount Road and take the

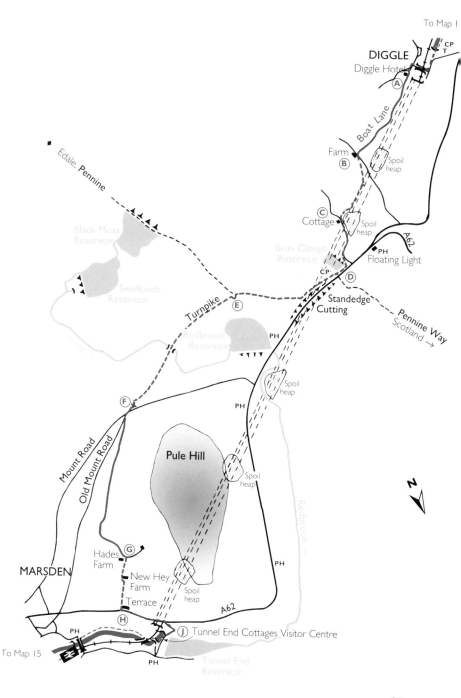

DIGGLE
Diggle Hotel

(A)

Boat Lane

Farm
(B)

Spoil heap

Edale, Pennine

Black Moss Reservoir

Cottage (C)

Spoil heap

A62

Brun Clough Reservoir

PH
Floating Light

Swellands Reservoir

CP

(D)

Standedge Cutting

Pennine Way
Scotland →

Turnpike (E)

Redbrook Reservoir

PH

Spoil heap

(F)

Mount Road

Old Mount Road

Pule Hill

PH

Spoil heap

Redbrook

Hades Farm (G)

MARSDEN

New Hey Farm

Terrace

Spoil heap

PH

A62

(H)

PH

(J) Tunnel End Cottages Visitor Centre

PH

Tunnel End Reservoir

N

87

unsurfaced lane veering left off this, signposted 'Hades Farm' and 'Standedge Trail'.

Below on the right is Butterley Reservoir, and this and others up the valley are for drinking water. There are splendid views across Marsden and down the Colne Valley towards Huddersfield.

After about a mile, the road swings to the left over a rise and drops down to Hades Farm. Turn right by the house [G], dropping straight down the steep hillside past New Hey Farm to the A62. Turn left on the main road [H] and then right on the first minor road [J].

At this junction, there is a splendid view over Tunnel End with the relationship of the three railway tunnels with the canal tunnel clearly visible. Tunnel End Reservoir can be seen, almost completely choked with silt and weeds, the overflow passing through sluices and over the top of the railway.

Follow the lane round to the right and, at the reservoir overflow, turn right over a stile on a footpath down to Tunnel End Cottages.

Additional Directions, Marsden to Diggle

Take the footpath behind Tunnel End Cottages up to the road. Follow the road left and up to the main road [J].

Head left, downhill on the A62 towards Marsden.

Look out for a long row of terraced houses on the right (Warrington Terrace) — take the footpath at the far end up the hill [H].

Keep straight up the track past the left-hand side of New Hey Farm.

At Hades Farm, take the track to the left [G].

Join Old Mount Road and, at Mount Road, cross straight over.

Take the footpath that drops down to and crosses a stream by a plank footbridge. Ascend the other side and a wooden post marks the start of the wide, grassy turnpike road [F].

At Brun Clough Reservoir, follow round the right-hand side alongside the A62, through the gate [D], then steeply down the path leading diagonally down the hillside to the cottage [C].

Pass the top of the spoil heaps and turn right down the footpath, keeping the curving boundary wall on your right.

At the farm [B], keep straight on down the gravel track to the Diggle Hotel [A].

Boat Lane and The Diggle Hotel

Standedge Tunnel Facts

At 5698 yards, Standedge Tunnel is the longest canal tunnel in Britain. It is also the deepest, more than 600 feet below ground. It is on the highest point of the waterways network, 650 feet above sea level.

Constructed between 1794 and 1811, it was proposed by Benjamin Outram with Nicholas Brown as surveyor. Setting out over two ridges with only surveying poles, telescope and string line resulted in the tunnel wandering 23 feet off its proposed centre-line. The Diggle end was also found to be higher than Marsden and the invert had to be lowered and the linings rebuilt. Thomas Telford was called in at a late date and expedited completion.

Side tunnels were built for construction of the railway tunnels, for the removal of spoil, bringing in construction materials and drainage. The tunnel was originally built with three passing places and another was added by the London & North Western Railway Company.

The canal tunnel was officially closed to through navigation in 1944, but has been nominally maintained to fulfil its drainage and water supply functions. Restoration of the tunnel is costed at more than £6 million and it is proposed to run underground boat trips in connection with the 'Standedge Experience' (see page 92) as well as through navigation.

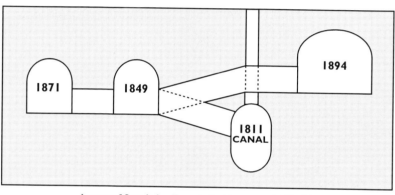

Layout of Standedge Tunnels (looking towards Diggle)

Diggle Portal

Standedge Tunnel

Alfred McAlpine
Civil Engineering

Alfred McAlpine
Civil Engineering (Eastern)
West Carr Road, Retford
Nottinghamshire, DN22 7SW

Tel: 01777 714200
Fax: 01777 714233

Alfred McAlpine
Civil Engineering (Western)
Exchange House, Kelburn Court
Leacroft Road, Birchwood
Warrington, WA3 6SY

Tel: 01925 858000
Fax: 01925 858099

Tunnel End, Marsden

British Waterways

**Caring for over 2000 miles
of Britain's Inland Waterways**

For further information please contact:-

HUDDERSFIELD NARROW CANAL PROJECT OFFICE

Tunnel End
Waters Road
Marsden
Huddersfield   HD7 6NQ
Tel: 01484 844298
Fax: 01484 847685

Map 15: *Huddersfield Narrow Canal*

Marsden to Slaithwaite

3 miles

Considering the magnitude of the engineering feat to drive a canal tunnel 3¼ miles deep through the Pennine hills, the portal at Tunnel End seems very much an understatement. Nevertheless, it is a very pretty place to visit, framed on one side by cottages, on the other by the railway and dwarfed by the high green hills all around.

Tunnel End Cottages are converted into a visitor centre (tel 01484 846062). Admission is free, and there are exhibitions about the canal and tunnels and also about the National Trust's Marsden Moor Estate. Huddersfield Canal Society's trip boat *Standedge Pioneer* operates trips from here. This is actually two boats, an unpowered 55-seat trip boat and a push-tug. As there is not always room to turn, the tug can be disconnected for a change in direction.

The large warehouse used to have a boat dock. It is to be converted into the 'Standedge Experience', a major heritage and visitor centre. Portakabins behind are the British Waterways project offices for the canal restoration scheme.

The summit pound is hemmed in on either side by heaps of spoil from the Standedge railway tunnels and much of it brought out by boat. Thankfully, nature has taken over and the area has mellowed into pleasant woodland. A picnic area has been made on the former railway sidings.

Immediately above Lock 42E, the current main water supply to the canal can be seen bubbling in. When the canal was abandoned in 1944 its channel was retained, supplying water to industrial users and to the Ashton and Huddersfield Broad Canals. The canal reservoirs between Marsden and Diggle now supply water to the public mains in Yorkshire, but by agreement, 9000 m³ per day is delivered to the canal, about 24 lockfulls in each direction.

The Top Lock 42E is convenient for the railway station and a good place from which to explore Marsden. The little town is built on the junction of two watercourses with a variety of weirs and interesting bridges. Near the church is a set of stocks. On Peel Street is the Mechanics Institute with its imposing tower, built in 1861 'to improve the intellect of the working classes'. So doing, it is now the home of Mikron Theatre, the well-known

theatre group set up by Mike and Sarah Lucas which tours the canal system during the summer on the narrow boat *Tysley*.

In May, Marsden Cuckoo Day celebrates a legend. The townspeople thought the cuckoo brought the summer. They tried to keep it in Marsden by building a wall round it but it wasn't tall enough: 'It were nobbut one course too low'!

The locks are close together through Marsden; some pounds are so short that they were built round to hold enough water. The canal hereabouts was dredged and the locks repaired in the late eighties and early nineties. Many of the chambers had been cascaded with their lower walls demolished.

At Sparth, the canal is trapped between a large mill dam and a reservoir which stores water from the locks above. The valley here is wide and the canal picturesque. Booth Lock 31E with its large turning basin and old lock cottage is a haven for ducks. It is a rewarding walk across the fields to the Olive Branch public house.

Canal and river enter a narrow, wooded gorge. Lock 24E marks the approach to Slaithwaite. The slipway at the head belongs to the Huddersfield Canal Society. Because the bridge at the lock tail has been widened, a guillotine gate has recently been fitted in place of bottom gates, one of three on this ring, but an unusual feature for a narrow canal.

Navigation Notes

This section is not normally navigated; contact Huddersfield Canal Society (0161 339 1332).

Towpath Notes

Good throughout.

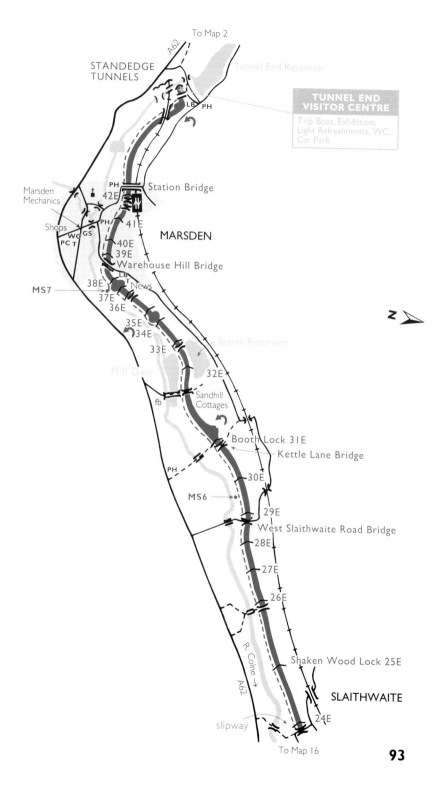

To Map 2

A62

STANDEDGE
TUNNELS

Tunnel End Reservoir

LB PH

**TUNNEL END
VISITOR CENTRE**
Trip Boat, Exhibition,
Light Refreshments, WC,
Car Park

Marsden
Mechanics

PH
42E   Station Bridge

Shops

PH
41E

Wo GS
PC T

MARSDEN

40E
39E

Warehouse Hill Bridge

LB
38E   News
MS7
37E
36E

35E
34E

33E

Sparth Reservoir

32E

Mill Dam

fb   Sandhill
Cottages

Booth Lock 31E
Kettle Lane Bridge

PH
30E

MS6
29E

West Slaithwaite Road Bridge

28E

27E

26E

R. Colne →

Shaken Wood Lock 25E

A62

SLAITHWAITE

24E

slipway

To Map 16

93

Tunnel End Cottages

Marsden Mechanics

Restaurant & Bar

94

Sparth Reservoir (nearest camera) and Cellars Clough Mill Dam

Booth Lock 31E

Map 16: *Huddersfield Narrow Canal*
Slaithwaite to Golcar
2 miles

The 5 milestone is in the gardens to the mill. The Moonraker Floating Tearoom is located on this pound, ideal to stop for a snack and support a canal-based business. From here, there is an attractive grouping of buildings, the sixteenth-century manor house with its mullioned windows, the former Free School, the Shoulder of Mutton pub and the parish church, all framed by the railway viaduct. Up the side valley beyond is Slaithwaite Reservoir, built originally by the Canal Company but now used by the local mills.

The Moonraker name comes from a local legend. Men threw cargoes off the moored boats into the canal to be collected later under the shadow of darkness. On one occasion, when apprehended by the law, the men pretended to be drunk and claimed to be trying to rake up the reflection of the moon from the canal.

Incidentally, the town name is not pronounced as it is written, but 'Slough-it' or even 'Slathwaite'. Slaithwaite has a good number of eating places, including a convenient fish and chip shop. The railway station is a short distance up the hill.

From Locks 23E to 21E, the canal has been infilled through Slaithwaite town centre. The route is not obstructed, though the humped Britannia Bridge has been demolished. Lock 22E is buried near to the toilet block on the public car park. The canal reappears at Lock 21E, where the pipe bringing water down the canal line has been broken through the head chamber. Below here, the locks have all been restored and the canal dredged.

Eastwards from Lock 20E, the canal has a rural feel once more in the wide valley bottom, though housing is now in preponderance on the hillsides. At regular intervals, there are weirs in the river followed by leats and mill dams behind the towpath. One of the oldest is Lowestwood Mills situated just above Lock 17E, where the canal has had to be squeezed into the hillside. In contrast, the massive Titanic Mills can be seen just across the fields. These were built in 1912 and steam-powered.

The bridge at Lowestwood Lane was widened in cast iron in 1884. At that time, the then owners of the canal, the London & North Western Railway Company, used the lozenge (diamond-shape) design on their railway wagons so that they could be identified by illiterate railway staff such as shunters.

The large field alongside Lock 16E at Linthwaite (the only large flat field in the valley), was the venue of the Inland Waterways Association's 1995 National Trailboat Festival. As there is no slipway, the 21 visiting small boats had to be craned into the canal and were able to cruise between the Lees Mill Bridge which has only 3 ft clearance and the fixed Holme Mills Swing Bridge.

Golcar Aqueduct carries the canal over the River Colne in a substantial single stone span. The gearing behind the towpath wall is a sluice which once fed water from the river above the weir through a culvert beneath the canal to the mills on the opposite bank.

Navigation Notes
Not normally navigated.

Towpath Notes
Good throughout.

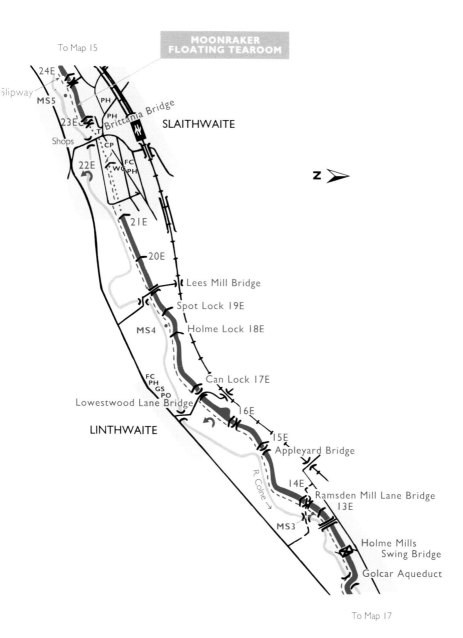

To Map 15

MOONRAKER
FLOATING TEAROOM

24E

Slipway

MS5

PH

PH

23E

Brittania Bridge

SLAITHWAITE

Shops

T

CP

22E

FC
WC
PH

21E

z

20E

Lees Mill Bridge

Spot Lock 19E

Holme Lock 18E

MS4

Can Lock 17E

FC
PH
GS
PO

16E

Lowestwood Lane Bridge

LINTHWAITE

15E

Appleyard Bridge

R. Colne →

14E

Ramsden Mill Lane Bridge

13E

MS3

Holme Mills
Swing Bridge

Golcar Aqueduct

To Map 17

Slaithwaite: Lock 23E

Linthwaite

Linthwaite

Holme Mills Swing Bridge

99

Map 17: *Huddersfield Narrow Canal*

Golcar to Huddersfield

3 miles

The canal skirts the foot of the steep north-facing and often wooded valley side; in winter the sun rarely penetrates down to the canal. From Milnsbridge the route into Huddersfield is urban, with mills and housing crammed into the narrow valley.

Milnsbridge is now a suburb of Huddersfield, but is a convenient shopping point. Views across the town are dominated by mills and the massive railway embankment. Up on the ridge is the stumpy Nab End Tower, built in 1861, a sort of Victorian 'Tower of Babel'.

Three locks of the Milnsbridge flight drop the canal past the Four Horseshoes public house to Milnsbridge Basin. Market Street Bridge was propped up for many years and has been renewed as part of the restoration. Down to Factory Street Bridge, a development of flats and inexpensive housing has been created by refurbishing the old Burdett and Union Mills and new building.

There are more diamond markings on Factory Lane Bridge (see page 96). Mark Bottoms Bridge has been demolished and infilled.

Below Birkhouse Bridge at milestone 1, the canal swings sharply to cross the River Colne on Paddock Aqueduct. Lock 5E is incorporated into the structure, the bywash commencing on the aqueduct. Directly overhead is the high railway viaduct on the Huddersfield-to-Barnsley line with its delicate-looking steel-trussed deck. The hump in the towpath marks a side arm beneath, but this does not penetrate the viaduct pier.

Much of the canal between Longroyd Bridge and Chapel Hill was infilled for redevelopment and the towpath is currently a dead end (see below). One blockage has been removed by diverting the canal onto the river bank in a concrete channel, making room for a Wickes DIY store. Buildings have been constructed across the canal by Sellars Engineering and work is in hand to overcome this blockage.

At Chapel Hill, the tail of Lock 3E can be seen in the car park. The canal and road bridge below are intact, but there is no access to this section.

Access to the towpath is regained at Queen Street Bridge. On the opposite side of the road, the new buildings built across the canal by Bates & Co. have been designed so that the canal can be restored beneath them.

Huddersfield University dominates the route to Aspley Basin. Mills behind the towpath are being converted into faculty buildings. The bend below Lock 1E marks the official end of the Huddersfield Narrow Canal.

The purpose-built university buildings treat the canal as an ornamental pond, and two old cranes have been retained in the landscaping. A notice proclaims Aspley Warehouse as the oldest surviving canal warehouse in the UK, being shown on a 1778 map. (While this is undoubtedly a notable building, older warehouses spring to mind such as West Stockwith on the Chesterfield Canal.) Opposite a water feeder enters the canal from the River Colne.

The Broad Canal above Wakefield Road Bridge was abandoned in 1963 and the bridge demolished. The new bridge, all seven highway lanes of it, was built by West Yorkshire County Council as a parting gesture with monies left over when it was wound up.

Navigation Notes

Narrow boats can penetrate Wakefield Road Bridge as far as Lock 1E (note low headroom), but beware of underwater obstructions in front of the University. Take care: this section is very shallow.

Towpath Notes

Longroyd Bridge to University

There is no through route east of Longroyd Bridge. Leave the towpath below the bridge, cross over the canal and head past The Electricians Arms. The new channel can be viewed from Wickes car park and Sellars Engineering blockage from the main road. Turn right down Chapel Hill to view Lock 3E. Continue down to the pedestrian crossing and turn left into Colne Road and first left again into Queen Street. Steps lead onto the towpath.

University to Longroyd Bridge

Leave the towpath up the steps and turn left. Turn right onto Colne Road. Cross Chapel Hill and turn right. Up the hill to the traffic lights, turn left onto Manchester Road and follow to Longroyd Bridge.

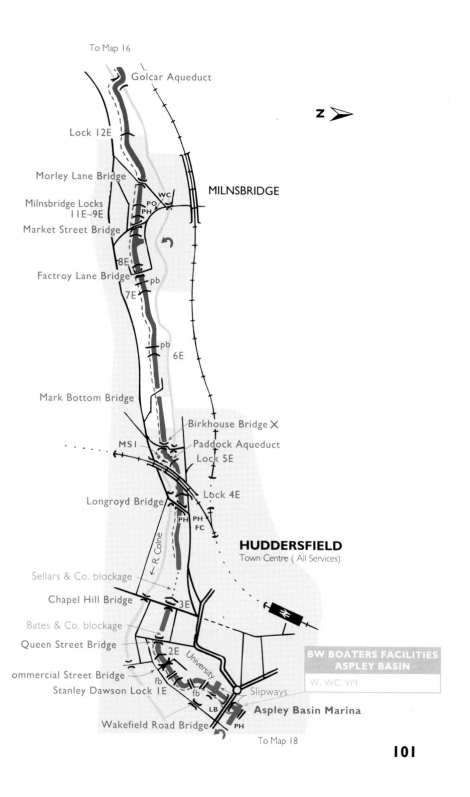

To Map 16

Golcar Aqueduct

Lock 12E

Morley Lane Bridge

MILNSBRIDGE

WC
PO
PH

Milnsbridge Locks
11E–9E

Market Street Bridge

8E

Factroy Lane Bridge

pb

7E

pb

6E

Mark Bottom Bridge

Birkhouse Bridge ✕

MS1

Paddock Aqueduct

Lock 5E

Lock 4E

Longroyd Bridge

PH PH
FC

HUDDERSFIELD
Town Centre (All Services)

R. Colne

Sellars & Co. blockage

Chapel Hill Bridge

3E

Bates & Co. blockage

Queen Street Bridge

2E

University

ommercial Street Bridge

fb

Stanley Dawson Lock 1E

fb

Slipways

Aspley Basin Marina

LB

PH

Wakefield Road Bridge

To Map 18

Lock 12E

Canal diversion for Wickes Superstore

History of The Huddersfield Broad Canal

The Huddersfield Broad Canal is perhaps more properly known as Sir John Ramsden's Canal for it was he (or rather his estate, because he was underage) that was the driving force behind it. The Ramsden Estate owned most of Huddersfield and was in the best position to gain advantage from the canal.

As soon as the Calder & Hebble Navigation was proposed, surveys were made for a canal up to Huddersfield, but it was not until 1774 that an Act was obtained, the canal opening two years later in 1776. Initially, it was very successful.

In 1845 the Broad Canal passed, with the Huddersfield Narrow, into railway ownership and traffic began slowly to decline. Following the closure of the Huddersfield Narrow in 1944, the Broad was sold to the Calder & Hebble Company. Commercial traffic ended in the 1950s, but the Broad was designated a Cruiseway under the 1968 Transport Act.

Huddersfield University

Map 18: *Huddersfield Broad Canal*

3 miles

Aspley Basin is a good mooring for boaters to visit Huddersfield. Some of the original warehouses still exist here, but much has been swept away in the name of new development. A large Sainsbury's store has created shoppers' moorings on its extensive waterfront.

Locomotive Bridge is the 'trademark' of the Huddersfield Broad Canal. Originally a swing bridge, the present unique lifting structure was built in 1865 to carry 'heavy road locomotives'.

Looking back, the tower on the hill is not a lighthouse for canal boaters coming up the canal, but the Jubilee Tower. It was built in 1898–99 to celebrate 60 years of Queen Victoria's reign. It is open to the public with splendid panoramic views all around (01484 223830; admission charge). It stands on top of Castle Hill, which has been occupied since the stone age, and the remains of an iron-age fort can still be seen. Across the valley, and over the roof tops, is Huddersfield Town Football Club's ultra-modern Sir Alfred McAlpine Stadium.

The landscape is better described as industrial rather than pretty as it leaves Huddersfield past the site of the old gasworks and the massive municipal incinerator. Tourism has even infiltrated here with the Grundy Mack Classic Cars Motor Museum next to Leeds Road Bridge.

The aspect changes with the locks. Now there are wide views across the Colne Valley, hillsides covered with woodland and bracken and playing fields either side of the canal.

Red Doles Lock has a lock cottage and stables. Most of the locks have arched bridges with no towpath below their bottom gates, which must have been very inconvenient in the days of horse haulage. Look carefully: handles remain on some where boatmen grabbed the towline as the boat emerged from the bridge; Lock 4 also has grooves cut by the rope in the rounded ends of the parapet and a metal bar on top to prevent the rope getting stuck between the copings.

Peacocks can be seen strolling at Lock 6; Huddersfield Community Urban Farm is on the lockside and visitors are welcome.

Beyond Leeds Road, the waterway is dominated by disused railway viaducts and a huge sewage works. Your researcher was not impressed by the 'phoney' heritage of cladding

huge modern treatment tanks in acres of unbroken sawn stonework.

Colne Bridge displays the date '1775' in its mellow stonework.

Cooper Bridge Lock 1 and its pretty cottage are dominated by a huge mill chimney. The lock discharges directly into the River Calder just upstream of a weir, so boaters have to take care when picking up their crew.

Navigation Notes

Locomotive Bridge requires a BW Watermate Key to operate. Once the key is turned, the road barriers are released and can be closed. (Watch out for road traffic.) The handle locking plate is now released and can be pushed in. All the above allows you to wind the handle in the good old-fashioned way to raise the bridge. The reverse procedure must be completed before the key is released.

Boaters must take particular care not to get swept onto the nearby weir when entering and leaving Cooper Bridge Lock 1. Coloured river level markers near the bottom gates indicate when it is safe to use the river: green = safe; orange = caution, red = do not proceed.

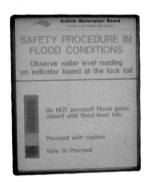

Towpath Notes

From Wakefield Road Bridge, climb the steps and turn left along the road, passing Aspley Wharf Marina and the basin end. A path behind The Aspley public house leads back to the towpath.

The river towpath from Cooper Bridge towards Brighouse is narrow and unsurfaced and can be slippery in wet weather.

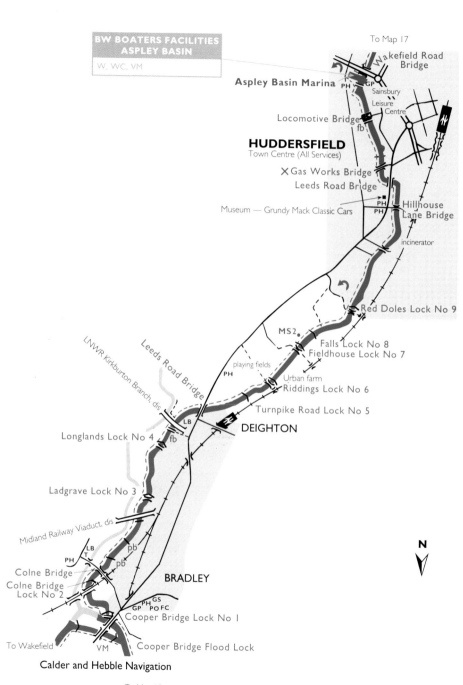

To Map 17

BW BOATERS FACILITIES
ASPLEY BASIN

W, WC, VM

Wakefield Road
Bridge

Aspley Basin Marina

PH   GP   Sainsbury

Leisure
Centre

Locomotive Bridge
fb

HUDDERSFIELD
Town Centre (All Services)

X Gas Works Bridge
Leeds Road Bridge

PH   Hillhouse
Lane Bridge
PH

Museum — Grundy Mack Classic Cars

incinerator

Red Doles Lock No 9

MS2

Falls Lock No 8
Fieldhouse Lock No 7

playing fields

PH

Urban farm

Riddings Lock No 6

Turnpike Road Lock No 5

DEIGHTON

LNWR Kirkburton Branch, dis

Leeds Road Bridge

LB
Longlands Lock No 4   fb

Ladgrave Lock No 3

Midland Railway Viaduct, dis

LB
T   pb
PH
pb

Colne Bridge
Colne Bridge
Lock No 2

BRADLEY

GS
GP PH PO FC
Cooper Bridge Lock No 1

To Wakefield   VM   Cooper Bridge Flood Lock

Calder and Hebble Navigation

N

To Map 19

Aspley Basin

Huddersfield

Locomotive Bridge

History of the Calder & Hebble Navigation

The merchants of Halifax cast envious eyes on their rivals in Wakefield and Leeds. The Rivers Aire and Calder had been made navigable from the Humber by 1720.

From 1740 proposals were made to extend navigation in the Calder to Salterhebble, and over the following years various plans were made and rejected. It was not until 1758 that an Act was obtained based on plans drawn up by John Smeaton. Subscribers from the Rochdale area realised how the scheme would benefit them, in receiving goods from Hull and wool from Lincolnshire, and added the section to Sowerby Bridge to connect with a new turnpike over the Pennines.

Construction started from Wakefield, reaching Brighouse in 1764 and Salterhebble a year later. Disastrous floods caused much damage and the navigation was closed for repairs. It was not until 1770 that Sowerby Bridge was finally reached.

From the start it was a highly successful business, and Parliament inserted a clause in the Act to limit the profits that could be made. The original navigation was not like the one we see today, but mostly a river navigation with short lock cuts. Within a few years, extensive improvements were made, bypassing difficult sections of river and increasing the depth so that heavier cargoes could be carried.

The company continued to be highly profitable until the coming of the Manchester & Leeds Railway. Through traffic was now threatened. There were arguments between the Aire & Calder, Rochdale, and Calder & Hebble Companies, and the shorter locks on the Calder & Hebble compounded the problem. Trade began to decline. Commercial traffic to Sowerby Bridge ceased by the mid-1950s, though coal carriage to Thornhill Power Station near Dewsbury survived into the 1980s. The navigation became a cruiseway under the 1968 Transport Act.

(For the history of the Halifax Canal, see page 118.)

Brighouse Locks

Map 19: *Calder & Hebble Navigation*
Cooper Bridge to Elland
4 miles

Cooper Bridge Flood Gates are seen in the far river bank. These are a single pair of gates which can be closed to protect the lock cut from river flooding. Conversely, they cannot be opened when the river rises and the navigation has to be closed. This was an unsatisfactory situation in the days of fly boats and commercial carrying, so most of the flood gates were upgraded to flood locks like that at Anchor Pit in the early nineteenth century. Ironically, Anchor Pit is now operated as flood gates, presumably to save the expense of a new pair of bottom gates.

Boaters passing through Cooper Bridge Flood Gates can follow the Calder & Hebble Navigation to Wakefield and the Aire & Calder Navigation to Selby or Goole, with connections to the rest of Britain's 3000 miles of connected waterways.

The river winds deep and wide to Kirklees Low Lock. The wooded slopes are Kirklees Park, grounds of Kirklees Priory where the famous outlaw Robin Hood is buried. According to legend Robin was ill and went to the prioress for help. She let his blood so liberally as a cure that he died, but not before he had shot an arrow to show where he should be buried. Amazingly, both the grave and the priory gatehouse, though listed buildings on land in public ownership, are not open to be visited.

Kirklees Cut is a peaceful place to moor or sit and rest. The island created between canal and river is being planted as 21 acres of natural woodland. On the cut there are many special features: a half-milepost and a hundred-yard post; LYR posts and unique Calder & Hebble paddle gear operated by handspike. Hundred-yard posts were set up above and below each lock and, if two boats arrived at the same time from opposite directions, then, when the boat horse arrived at the post, the whip was cracked to claim right of passage for its crew (presumably irrespective of how the lock was set). This was supposed to prevent fisticuffs between rival boat crews. Posts marked 'LYR' are boundary markers indicating the canal was once leased by the Lancashire & Yorkshire Railway Company.

The navigation returns to the river at Anchor Pit Flood Lock. A row of bright orange rollers across the river are meant to stop boats from being swept onto the weir while allowing flotsam and jetsam free passage downstream. This tawdry length of river is bounded by wire fences, the rear of factories and British Car Auctions. The towpath is virtually non-existent (see below).

Two locks lift the navigation out of the river for the last time — from Brighouse to Sowerby Bridge is all canal. There are visitor moorings in the almost circular pound between the locks and, above, another basin filled with colourful moored boats is complemented by an early warehouse now used by Sagar boat-builders. The 3 ft-gauge Clifton Colliery Tramway brought coal here from the Clifton area until the 1920s. There has been mining in the area since the fourteenth century.

Brighouse, with a population of 35,000, is clearly proud of its canal, and valiant efforts have been made, giving the towpath a promenade feel. Close to the basin there is a pub and an excellent Italian restaurant. There are further moorings next to Anchor Bridge which are convenient for shopping, the market, Tesco, the swimming baths, the bus station and The Black Bull public house.

By Huddersfield Road Bridge, there is a horse recovery ramp from the towpath into the canal: Boat horses scared by noisy town traffic occasionally fell into the water and it was otherwise impossible to get them out over the stone bank.

At Ganny Lock, the navigation formerly returned to the river and the lock cottage sits on top of the old river lock. With wooded cliffs on one hand and the towpath dividing canal from river on the other, a stream tumbling into the canal ahead, this is a very attractive section. At Brookfoot, a set of old flood gates leading to the river are now blocked off; these allowed vessels to gain access to premises on the farther bank of the old river navigation.

Water-skiing takes place on the lake alongside Cromwell Lock, and there are two naturist clubs on the hillside beyond. There are picnic benches on an old wharf at Rawson's Pool, accessible only to boaters. The Colliers Arms has excellent moorings for patrons.

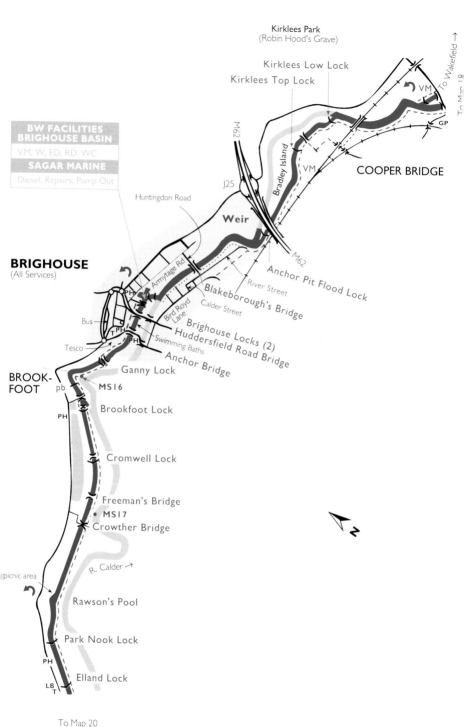

Kirklees Park
(Robin Hood's Grave)

Kirklees Low Lock

Kirklees Top Lock

To Wakefield →

To Map 18

VM

GP

COOPER BRIDGE

Bradley Island

VM

M62

J25

Huntingdon Road

Weir

Anchor Pit Flood Lock

M62

BW FACILITIES BRIGHOUSE BASIN
VM, W, ED, RD, WC
SAGAR MARINE
Diesel, Repairs, Pump Out

BRIGHOUSE
(All Services)

Armytage Rd

River Street

Blakeborough's Bridge

Calder Street

Bird Royd Lane

Brighouse Locks (2)

Huddersfield Road Bridge

PH

Bus

PH

Tesco

PH

Swimming Baths

Anchor Bridge

BROOK-FOOT

pb

MS16

Ganny Lock

PH

Brookfoot Lock

Cromwell Lock

Freeman's Bridge

● MS17

Crowther Bridge

R. Calder →

picnic area

Rawson's Pool

Park Nook Lock

PH

LB
T

Elland Lock

To Map 20

N

109

Navigation Notes

Boaters approaching the Huddersfield Broad Canal must take care not to be swept onto the weir.

There are good visitor moorings on the Calder & Hebble Navigation inside Cooper Bridge Flood Gates.

Coloured river level markers at the river locks indicate when it is safe to use the river: green = safe; orange = caution, river above normal level; red = do not proceed. It will not be possible to open Cooper Bridge Flood Gates or Anchor Pit Flood Lock if levels are significantly raised. Water levels can rise and fall very quickly. The bottom gates of Anchor Pit Flood Lock are inoperative.

Towpath Notes

The first few hundred yards of river path from Cooper Bridge are narrow and unsurfaced and can be slippery in wet weather.

The towpath bridge over the river at Brighouse Low Lock is missing and the towpath to Anchor Pit Flood Lock is badly overgrown. The walker is required to make a depressing diversion via River Street. Turn right at the black and yellow barriers and cross the concrete river bridge. Turn left along Armytage Road to Brighouse Basin. (Your intrepid researcher got terribly scratched by brambles when he walked the towpath as far as Calder St.)

Brighouse Basin

THE COLLIERS ARMS

Park Road, Elland

Mine Hosts: Peter & Nanette Kingston

Opening hours

Mon–Fri: 11.00am–3.00pm; 5.30–11.00pm; Sat: 11.00am–11.00pm; Sun: 12.00–10.30pm
Hot & Cold Meals: Daily: 12.00–2.00pm; Thur–Fri: 6.00–8.00pm; Sun: 6.30–8.30pm

❖ **COSY LOUNGE**   ❖ **SNUG AREA**   ❖ **PUBLIC BAR**
❖ **BEER GARDEN**   ❖ **HOT & COLD MEALS (CHILDREN'S MENU)**
❖ **CONSERVATORY**   ❖ **AMPLE VISITOR MOORINGS (24 HRS)**

A friendly welcome guaranteed

Pleasant overnight moorings at The Colliers' Arms, Elland

Map 20: *Calder & Hebble Navigation*
Elland to Sowerby Bridge
4¹/₂ miles

Elland Wharf is a time capsule in a modern world. It is enclosed by the Wharf House, a warehouse restored as offices, wharf buildings and the Barge & Barrel pub. Visitor Moorings here are ideal for exploring into the little town with its market charter dating back to 1317. The shopping centre with its Co-op supermarket and swimming pool is a pleasant half-mile walk over the old river bridge, up North-gate past the twelfth-century parish church and along Southgate. Friday is market day.

The canal is picturesque as it skirts Elland Wood Bottom. At Woodside Mills Lock, elegant arched stonework and mooring rings are all that remains of a massive flour mill once served by water.

The three locks at Salterhebble are attractively landscaped and full of interest, a popular spot for gongoozlers. The bottom chamber has a guillotine gate as a result of road-widening. This leads directly into a small aqueduct over the Hebble Brook which, until recent replacement, was made of wood. James Brindley spent a short period here as engineer during construction of the canal. He arranged the top two locks as a staircase, but this was found to be unsatisfactory. The top chamber is probably part of the original staircase, explaining the strange shape of the short pound between the locks.

At the top of the locks is the junction for Halifax or Sowerby Bridge. Turning right, a quarter of mile of canal leads to moorings for The Quays public house and a dry dock. This was the site of the original wharf built to serve Halifax, goods having to be carted 1¹/₂ miles up the steep hill to town, before the Halifax Canal was constructed (see page 118).

Turning left, the scenery to Sowerby Bridge is dominated by the steep craggy rise of Norland Moor across the wide valley. At Copley, the Halifax-to-Sowerby Bridge railway spans the valley on 23 arches. At Stern Mills Bridge, there are glimpses to the right of the Halifax Building Society's Computer Department, a truly massive building.

Up on the hill above, Wainhouse Tower dominates the landscape. Built as a chimney for a dyeworks, it was never used as such. Quite why it was built with stairs, a viewing gallery and ornate stonework is not known. Local legend says that, when a neighbour built a high wall round his garden and boasted that no one could see into it, J.E. Wainhouse put up his tower and opened it to the public! The tower is open on occasional Sundays and Bank Holidays (01422 359454; admission charge).

The canal sneaks quietly into Sowerby Bridge under a procession of small bridges. Before the basin, the Rochdale Canal swings off to the left. Warehouses were erected here almost as soon as the canal opened in 1770 and further building arose with the opening of the Rochdale Canal and the transhipment that took place as a result of the differing lock lengths. Now the warehouses have been put to a variety of uses, including Shire Cruisers Boat Hire, craft workshops and The Moorings pub. The large building on the right was Bolton Brow Methodist Chapel (its main claim to fame being that your researcher was married there).

Before 1760 there was a small population in the Sowerby Bridge area, centred on the mediaeval bridge over the Calder. Over the next 70 years the town grew rapidly with the coming of the canal, turnpike roads, the railway and the industrial revolution. Manufacture of textiles changed from a cottage industry, first to water- and then to steam-powered mills. Mill engines manufactured in Sowerby Bridge were exported worldwide.

By the 1970s, the town had become rather run down and derelict. Now a resurgence of local pride has resulted in old mills in the town centre being redeveloped, the making of a canoe slalom course on the river and the reopening of the Rochdale Canal. The boat rally celebrating the opening of Tuel Lane Lock in May 1996 seems to have become an annual event and the rushbearing festival in autumn has been revived.

From the basin, most of the shops are along Wharf Street, turn left out of the basin or walk up the two Rochdale Locks. There are many places of refreshment, and a small market is held Tuesday, Friday and Saturday just over the river bridge.

Navigation Notes

Salterhebble guillotine gate is operated using a BW Watermate Key. Ensure the top gates are fully closed before operating.

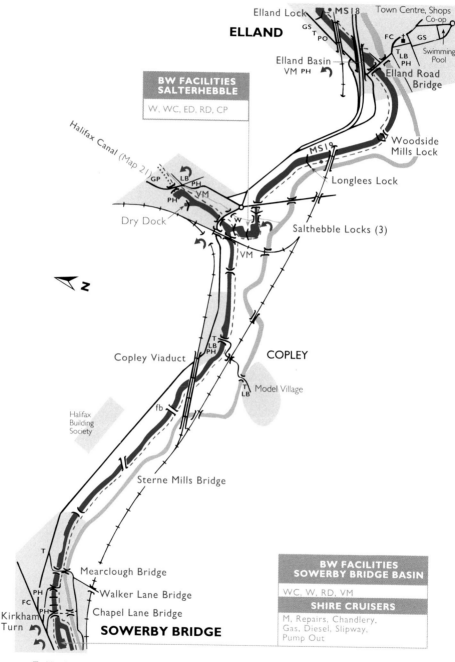

To Map 19

Elland Lock
MS18
Town Centre, Shops
Co-op

ELLAND

GS
T PO

FC
GS

T
LB
PH

Swimming
Pool

Elland Basin
VM PH

Elland Road
Bridge

Halifax Canal (Map 21)

**BW FACILITIES
SALTERHEBBLE**

W, WC, ED, RD, CP

MS19

Woodside
Mills Lock

GP
LB
PH

VM

Longlees Lock

PH

Dry Dock

W

Salthebble Locks (3)

VM

N

Copley Viaduct

T
LB
PH

COPLEY

T
LB

Model Village

fb

Halifax
Building
Society

Sterne Mills Bridge

T

Mearclough Bridge

PH

FC

Walker Lane Bridge

PH

Chapel Lane Bridge

Kirkham
Turn

SOWERBY BRIDGE

**BW FACILITIES
SOWERBY BRIDGE BASIN**

WC, W, RD, VM

SHIRE CRUISERS

M, Repairs, Chandlery,
Gas, Diesel, Slipway,
Pump Out

To Map 1

Towpath Notes

At Elland Wharf, the bridge that should carry the towpath over the canal is missing. From the Sowerby Bridge direction, leave the towpath before the Barge & Barrel public house and cross over Elland Road Bridge. Turn left down the lane that runs along the back of the wharf. Past the warehouse and Wharf House, a cobbled path leads onto the towpath.

Salterhebble Locks

Elland Wharf and the Barge & Barrel Visitor Moorings

Elland Wood Bottom

Sowerby Bridge

Kirkham Turn

Float Free

Explore the waterways in this guide and beyond with Yorkshire's leading fleet of self-drive holiday boats.

Or bring your own boat to us for moorings, hard standing, boat repairs, diesel engine maintenance, gas fitting (Corgi registered).

Member of the British Marine INDUSTRIES FEDERATION

Shire Cruisers

The Wharf, Sowerby Bridge, HX6 2AG
Telephone: 01422 832712
(Fax: 01422 839565)

YORKSHIRE TOURIST BOARD MEMBER

Shire Cruisers

Map 21
A Walk up the Halifax Branch Canal
1 1/2 miles

The Halifax Branch of the Calder & Hebble Navigation opened in 1828. Fourteen locks raised the canal 100 feet to the town's terminal basin. The route closely follows that of the Hebble Brook but, because of the many water mills, the company was only allowed to take a water supply from the lower end — hence all water had to be pumped. Water was taken near Lock 1 and passed through a 1200-yard-long tunnel to a pump house operated by a beam engine. It was then pumped to a reservoir which has long since been built on. Not surprisingly, the canal was expensive to operate and the toll charges high. The branch was abandoned during the Second World War.

Calderdale Town Planning Department has constructed a footpath using parts of the route entitled the 'Hebble Trail'. Much of this is incorporated in the walk on this page, but I have included more of the canal route for the benefit of the enthusiast. After all these years, it is surprising how much of the navigation still remains.

Outside The Quays public house, a footpath has been created through the canal bridge and the chamber of Lock 1. On the right can be seen a leat and chambers which divert water from the Hebble into the canal. To avoid the garden of Myrtle Cottage with its mock suspension bridge, the path diverts round the left-hand side of Lock 2, before crossing over the head of the chamber on a wooden footbridge. The towpath can now be followed and the shape of the dry canal can be seen for a short distance before tipping entirely buries the channel area.

Crossing the narrow cobbled road, the parapets of the bridge at the tail of Lock 3 can still be seen. The path continues on the river bank, the fenced compound being the infilled site of two very short and wide pounds above and below Lock 4.

Ahead is a substantial aqueduct over the Hebble Brook which incorporated the head of Lock 5. The path crosses the aqueduct and soon the coping stones of infilled Lock 6 are encountered. At Lock 7, a seat has been provided under the accommodation bridge, and the lock walls are visible.

Infilling makes it difficult to guess the location of Lock 8 and, beyond, the path is diverted up onto the road. A diversion should be taken up Phoebe Lane to the right. The pumping station beam engine house is found at the junction at the top of the hill and is now used as a car workshop. The attendant's cottage next door is very reminiscent of Salterhebble lock cottage.

Return down the hill to the canal. Again the bridge parapets are still in place and the position of Lock 9 can be seen. The canal to Lock 10 is lightly filled, but is on private property and there is no exit at the far end. Therefore, divert down Phoebe Lane over the brook, right, up the stone-setted footpath and along Shaw Lane. Turn right down Boys Lane past The Shears public house and right again on Whitegates Road to reach the canal.

Once again, the bridge is in situ, and traces of Lock 10 can be found. Follow the footpath along the river bank. This ran below the retaining wall that held up the canal towpath. Lock 11 was situated where the cul-de-sac road crosses the brook. A factory has been built over the canal, with a footpath tunnel through. Beyond, a short stretch of canal remains, though tipping and demolition rubble are all around. The towpath and copings, a wharf on the far bank and Water Lane Bridge can still be seen.

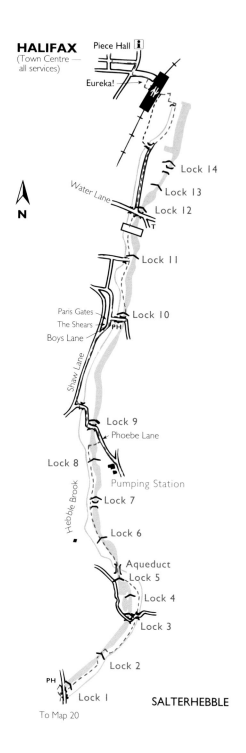

HALIFAX
(Town Centre —
all services)

Piece Hall ℹ️

Eureka!

N

Lock 14

Water Lane

Lock 13

Lock 12

T

Lock 11

Paris Gates
The Shears
Boys Lane

PH

Lock 10

Shaw Lane

Lock 9

Phoebe Lane

Lock 8

Pumping Station

Hebble Brook

Lock 7

Lock 6

Aqueduct
Lock 5

Lock 4

Lock 3

Lock 2

PH

Lock 1

SALTERHEBBLE

To Map 20

119

Steps lead up to Water Lane and the remainder of the canal route cannot be followed as a large confectionery factory has been built upon it. Follow the lane ahead, which turns into a footpath cantilevered over the stream on large stone slabs. The retaining wall was built to support the canal basin when this was extended out to the brook.

To reach the town centre, head for the bridge beneath the railway station which emerges next to the Eureka! museum. The road ahead leads past the Piece Hall to the town centre where a bus can be caught back to Salterhebble.

Halifax

A substantial Yorkshire woollen town with extensive shopping area in the elegant Victorian town centre. There are traffic-free areas, arcades and the lively Borough Market dating from 1896 is a grade I listed building.

Halifax Piece Hall

An elegant galleried and colonnaded eighteenth-century building surrounds the four sides of what was originally the marketplace for the cottage weaving industry. Now it houses the tourist information office, craft and speciality shops, a restaurant and a museum. Markets are held Thursday, Friday and Saturday.

Eureka!

Eureka! is a museum of discovery for children. It has won many awards and is very popular. It teaches about many aspects of life by allowing children to hands-on access to the exhibits and experiments. Admission charge.

Above Lock 2

Aqueduct over the Hebble Brook

Halifax Branch

The Quays, Salterhebble

Public Transport

The South Pennine Ring is well served by bus and train, allowing the walker to explore a length of canal and return by public transport, or the boater to explore more of the route than it is presently possible to navigate. Many people (the author included) walk the whole route in this way.

Remember that not all services operate on a Sunday.

Greater Manchester

All local bus and train times are available from the Greater Manchester Passenger Transport Executive Enquiry Line (0161 228 7811).

Manchester Piccadilly and Victoria stations are connected by a frequent tram service: Metrolink (0161 205 2000).

Note that Calder Valley trains from north and east of Rochdale do not stop between Rochdale and Manchester.

Useful bus services include:

Greenfield Station–Uppermill–Woolroad– Diggle
Greenfield Station–Uppermill–Woolroad– Marsden

West Yorkshire

All local bus and train times are available Metro (the brand name of West Yorkshire Passenger Transport Executive; 0113 242 7676).

In addition to the rail services, there are frequent bus services parallel to the canal in the Calder and Colne Valleys

Of particular interest to transport enthusiasts will be the services operated by Halifax Joint Committee:

Hebden Bridge–Sowerby Bridge–Halifax
Hebden Bridge–Sowerby Bridge– Salterhebble–Elland–Huddersfield

This small company set out using a vintage Halifax Corporation bus, and now operates a small fleet of bright orange and green vehicles with open platforms and conductors. Times from Metro (above) or 01422 343557.

National Train Enquiries

In addition to the information offered by the Passenger Transport Executives (above), train times can be obtained on 0345 484950.

Railway Services

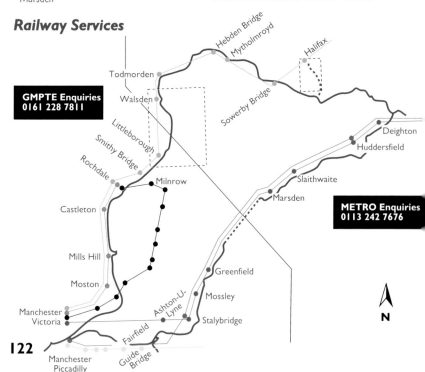

GMPTE Enquiries
0161 228 7811

METRO Enquiries
0113 242 7676

N

Public Houses

Map	Location	Distance from canal (yards)	Pub name	Telephone	Evening meal	Lunch	Children	Beer garden	B&B
Rochdale Canal									
1	Tuel Lane Lock	0	Lockkeeper's Tavern	01422 832701					
1	Sowerby Embankment	100	Puzzle Hall Inn	01422 835547	✓	✓		✓	
1	Luddenden Foot	50	The Weaver's Arms	01422 882241					
1	Luddenden Foot	100	Coach & Horses	01422 884102	✓	✓	✓		
1	Brearley	200	The Grove Inn	01422 844650	✓	✓	✓	✓	
2	Mytholmroyd	0	White Lion	01422 883131		✓	✓	✓	
2	Mytholmroyd	100	Dusty Miller	01422 882247		✓	✓		
2	Mytholmroyd Station	400	Shoulder of Mutton	01422 883165	✓	✓	✓	✓	
2	Mayroyd Bridge	50	Thirsty Turtle	01422 846064	✓	✓	✓	✓	
2	Hebden Bridge Marina	0	The Railway	01422 844088		✓	✓		
2	Stubbing Wharf	0	Stubbing Wharf	01422 844107	✓	✓	✓	✓	
2	Rawden Mill Lock	150	The Woodman*	01422 842458	✓	✓	✓	✓	✓
3	Lob Mill Lock	300	Rose & Crown	01706 812428	✓	✓	✓		
3	Shop Lock	150	Duke of York	01706 815770	✓	✓	✓	✓	
3	Library Lock	0	Golden Lion	01706 813532	✓	✓	✓	✓	
3	Library Lock	0	Bramsche Continental Bar	01706 815117		✓	✓		
3	Gauxholme Highest	50	Mason's Arms	01706 812180	✓	✓			
3	Hollins Lock	100	Hollins Inn	01706 817105	✓	✓	✓		
3	Travis Mill Lock	0	Cross Keys	01706 815185	✓	✓	✓	✓	✓
4	Warland Swing Bridge	150	Bird i'th Hand	01706 378145	✓	✓	✓		
4	Summit West Lock	0	The Summit	01706 378011	✓	✓	✓	✓	
4	Lock 39	50	The Sportsman's Rest	01706 377741		✓	✓		
4	Durn Bridge	100	The Rake Inn	01706 379689	✓	✓	M	✓	
4	Canal Road Bridge	0	Waterside Inn	01706 376250		✓	✓	✓	✓
5	Reservoirs Walk	0	The White House	01706 378456	✓	✓	✓		
5	Hollingworth Lake	0	Fishermen's Inn	01706 378168	✓	✓			
5	Hollingworth Lake	750	The Beach	01706 378163	✓	✓	✓	✓	
6	Milnrow Road Bridge	50	Lord Nelson	01706 359549					
6	Rochdale Arm	50	Prince Albert	01706 642305					✓
7	Wellith Lane Bridge	15	Horse & Jockey	01706 646426		✓			
7	Castleton	50	Blue Pits Inn	01706 632151					
7	Castleton	50	The Bridge Inn	01706 650552	✓	✓	✓		
7	Above Slattocks Top	0	Hopwood Arms	01706 645948	✓	✓	✓	✓	
7	Lock 55	0	Ship Inn	N/A					
7	Mill Hill	0	The Rose of Lancaster	0161 5243031	✓	✓	✓	✓	
8	Foxdenton Lane Bridge	50	The Railway & Linnet	0161 6432047	✓	✓	✓	✓	✓

* Camping facilities   M: Children allowed when having meal

Public Houses *(continued)*

Map	Location	Distance from canal (yards)	Pub name	Telephone	Evening meal	Lunch	Children	Beer garden	B&B
8	Foxdenton Lane Bridge	150	Radclyffe Arms	0161 6432790	✓	✓	✓	✓	✓
8	Broadway	0	The Boat & Horses	0161 6812363	✓				
8	Failsworth	0	Bridge Inn	0161 6823033		✓		✓	
8	Newton Heath	0	New Crown Inn	0161 6834218		✓		✓	
9	Lock 80	0	The Navigation	N/A					
9	Sackville Street Bridge	0	The Rembrandt	0161 2361311	✓	✓	M	✓	✓
9	Princess Street Lock 87	0	New Union Inn	0161 2281492					
9	Lock 92	0	Dukes 92	0161 8398646	✓	✓	✓	✓	
Ashton Canal									
10	Lock 9	0	Bridge Inn	0161 2232878					
10	Lock 13	0	The Strawberry Duck	0161 2234415	✓	✓	M	✓	
10	Lock 15	50	The Friendship	0161 3702111		✓		✓	
10	Bridge 19	0	The Causeway	0161 3015680	✓	✓	✓	✓	
10	Guide Bridge	0	The Boundary	0161 3301679	✓	✓	✓	✓	
10	Guide Bridge	0	Corporation Arms	0161 3302070	✓	✓	M	✓	
Huddersfield Narrow									
11	Peel Street Bridge	50	The Feathers	0161 3386403			✓	✓	
11	Staley Wharf	0	The Barge	0161 3382964			✓	✓	
11	Staley Wharf	0	Wharf Tavern	N/A					
11	Staley Wharf	0	The Wellington	N/A					
12	Wagon Road Bridge	50	New Bridge Inn	01457 832146	✓		✓	✓	
12	Roaches Lock	0	Roaches Lock	01457 834288	✓	✓	✓	✓	
12	Lock 16W	50	Tollemache Arms	01457 832354	✓	✓	✓	✓	✓
12	Chew Valley Road Bridge	100	The Railway Hotel	01457 872307				✓	✓
12	Uppermill Wade Lock	50	Granby Arms	01457 872348		✓	✓	✓	
12	Uppermill Wade Lock	100	The Waggon	01457 872376		✓	✓		
13	Wool Road Bridge	100	The Navigation	01457 872418	✓	✓	✓		
14	Boat Lane, Diggle	0	Diggle Hotel	01457 872741	✓	✓	✓	✓	✓
14	Brun Clough	100	Floating Light	01457 874242	✓	✓	✓	✓	✓
14	Tunnel Top A62	0	Great Western	01484 844315	✓	✓		✓	
15	Tunnel End	100	Tunnel End Inn	01484 844636					
15	Marsden Station	0	Railway Hotel	01484 844417	✓	✓	✓	✓	✓
15	Booth Lock 31E	300	Olive Branch	01484 844487	✓	✓	✓		✓

Public Houses *(continued)*

Map	Location	Distance from canal (yards)	Pub name	Telephone	Facilities				
					Evening meal	Lunch	Children	Beer garden	B&B
16	Lock 24E	150	Silent Woman	01484 842819		✓	✓	✓	
16	Lock 24E	0	Shoulder of Mutton	01484 842228		✓	✓		
16	Britannia Bridge	0	The Commercial	01484 842920			✓		
16	Lock 23E	100	The Pack Horse	01484 844690			✓		✓
17	Lock 10E	6	Four Horseshoes	01484 653550			✓	✓	
17	Manchester Road Bridge	50	Electricians Arms	01484 429779	✓		✓		
	Huddersfield Broad								
18	Aspley Basin	0	The Aspley	01484 544250	✓	✓	✓		
18	Millhouse Lane Bridge	100	Market Tavern	01484 420452		✓	✓		
18	Millhouse Lane Bridge	100	Spinner's Arms	01484 421062	✓	✓	✓		
18	Lock No. 5	300	White Horse Inn	01484 423899	✓		✓	✓	
18	Colne Bridge	200	The Royal & Ancient	01484 425461	✓	✓			
18	Cooper Bridge	200	White Cross Inn	01484 306206	✓	✓	✓	✓	
	Calder & Hebble								
19	Brighouse Basin	100	The Barge	N/A					
19	Anchor Bridge	0	New Anchor Inn	01422 823545		✓	✓		
19	Anchor Bridge	50	Black Swan	01484 712006			✓		
19	Anchor Bridge	50	Black Bull	01484 714816	✓	✓	✓	✓	✓
19	Brookfoot Lock	450	Lakeside Lodge	01484 713049	✓	✓	✓	✓	✓
19	Above Park Nook Lock	0	Collier's Arms	01422 372704	✓	✓	✓	✓	
19	Elland Lock	100	Sacha Court Hotel	01422 377232	✓	✓		✓	
20	Elland Wharf	0	Barge and Barrel	01422 373623	✓	✓	✓	✓	
20	Elland Wharf	150	The Royal	01422 378406		✓			
20	Elland Wharf	150	Malt Shovel	01422 373189		✓			
20	Halifax Branch	0	The Quays	01422 347700	✓	✓	✓	✓	✓
20	Halifax Branch	0	The Punch Bowl	01422 366937			✓	✓	✓
21	Hebble Trail	0	Shears Inn	01422 362936		✓			
21	Copley	50	Volunteer Arms	01422 360723		✓	✓	✓	
21	Chapel Lane Bridge	0	The Navigation	01422 831636	✓	✓	✓	✓	✓
21	Sowerby Bridge Basin	0	The Moorings	01422 833940	✓	✓	✓	✓	
21	Sowerby Bridge Basin	50	The Ash Tree	01422 831654	✓		✓	✓	

Further Information

Navigation Authorities

British Waterways
Headquarters and craft licensing: Willow Grange, Church Road, Watford WD1 3QA, 01923 226422

Waterway Manager, Calder & Hebble Navigation and Huddersfield Broad Canal: Lock Lane, Castleford, West Yorkshire WF10 2LH, 01977 554351

Waterway Manager, Ashton Canal, Peak Forest, Huddersfield Narrow: Top Lock, Church Lane, Marple SK6 6BN, 0161 427 1079

Huddersfield Narrow Canal Project, Marsden, 01484 844298

Rochdale Canal Company (Manchester Nine Locks): 75, Dale Street, Manchester M1 2HG, 0161 236 2456

Rochdale Canal Trust (Sowerby Bridge to Littleborough, etc.): Callis Mill, Charles Town, Hebden Bridge, 01422 844990

Bridgewater Canal
Manchester Ship Canal Company, 7th Floor, Quay West, Trafford Wharf Road, Manchester, M17 1HH, 0161 872 2411

Boating Contacts

Shire Cruisers (boatyard, moorings, fuel, pump-out): Sowerby Bridge 01422 832712

Tuel Lane lock-keeper: 01422 316678

Pickwell & Arnold (boat-builders, fuel, pump-out): Todmorden, 01706 812411

Baltimore Marina (pump-out, moorings): 01706 816472

Egerton Narrowboats (boatyard, moorings, fuel): Castlefield, 0161 833 9878

Warble Narrowboats (boatyard): Hyde, Peak Forest Canal, 0161 367 9205

Aspley Wharf Marina (boat sales, chandlery): 01484 514123

Mirfield Boatyard (boatyard, fuel, pump-out): 01924 492007

Heron Boatshare: 0500 585829

Sagar Marine (boat-builders, fuel, pump-out, moorings): Brighouse, 01484 714541

Tayberg Steel Boats (boat-builders): 01484 400221

Canal Societies/Waterway Groups

Inland Waterways Association
114, Regents Park Road, London NW1 8UQ, 0171 586 2556/2510

Rochdale Canal Society
3, The Broad Ing, Passmonds, Rochdale OL12 7AR, 01706 646132

Huddersfield Canal Society
239, Mossley Road, Ashton-under-Lyne OL6 6LN, 0161 339 1332

Calder Navigation Society
The Dene, Triangle, Sowerby Bridge HX6 3EA, 01422 823562

Hire Boats

Shire Cruisers (Sowerby Bridge): 01422 832712

Pickwell & Arnold (Todmorden): 01706 812411

Baltimore Boats (Todmorden): 01706 816472

Egerton Narrowboats (Manchester): 0161 833 9878

Shepley Bridge Marina (Calder & Hebble): 01924 491872

Trip Boats

Cassoulet Restaurant Boat (Sowerby Bridge): 01422 353708/0973 419733

Calder Valley Cruising (Hebden Bridge; horse-drawn): 01422 845557

Bridgewater Packet Boat Service: 0161 748 2680/0802 476407

Oldham Otter (Ashton Canal Bridge 19): 0161 339 1332

Ashton Packet Boat Co. (Guide Bridge; horse-drawn): 0161 320 8338

Greater Manchester (Ashton-under-Lyne): 0161 339 1332

Pennine Moonraker (Uppermill): 0161 683 5728/01457 873085

Pioneer (Tunnel End): 0161 339 1332

Savile (Calder Navigation Society; see above)

Waylon (Brighouse): 01484 713424

Tourist Information

Halifax (Piece Hall): 01422 368725

Hebden Bridge (1 Bridge Gate): 01422 843831

Todmorden (15 Burnley Rd): 01706 818181

Littleborough (Coach House): 01706 378481

Rochdale (Clock Tower, Town Hall): 01706 356592

Oldham: 0161 627 1024

Manchester (Town Hall Extension): 0161 234 3157

Castlefield Visitor Centre: 0161 834 4026

Ashton-under-Lyne (32 Market Street): 0161 343 4343

Uppermill (Saddleworth Museum): 01457 874093

Brownhill Visitor Centre: 01457 872598

Tunnel End Cottages: 01484 846062

Huddersfield: 01484 223200

Tourist Attractions, etc.
(alphabetical order)

Bridgewater Hall: 0161 907 9000

Daisy Nook Countryside Centre: 0161 620 8202

East Lancashire Railway: 0161 764 7790

Ellenroad Engine House: 01706 881952

Eureka! Museum for Children (Halifax): 01422 330012

Granada Studio Tours: 0161 832 4999

Grundy Mack Motor Museum: 01484 450446

Hebden Bridge Cinema: 01422 842807

Hollingworth Lake Country Park: 01706 373421

Mikron Theatre: 01484 843701

Museum of Science & Industry in Manchester: 0161 832 1830

National Trust, Marsden Moor Estate: 01484 847016

Portland Basin Heritage Centre: 0161 339 2906

Pumphouse Museum, Castlefield: 0161 839 6061

Rochdale Pioneers Museum: 01706 524920

Walkley's Clogs, Hebden Bridge: 01422 842061

Index